The Illustrated
ATLAS
OF THE
Bible Lands

Warwick Press

Above: Mount Ararat in Turkey, the traditional site of the grounding of Noah's Ark. It is a volcano 5185 m (17,011 ft) high.

Left: Mosaic of the seven-branched candlestick or menorah. *A golden* menorah *stood in the Tabernacle, the Jew's first Holy Temple. The seven branches are supposed to represent the Sun, Moon and five planets known to antiquity.*

Endpapers: A 6th-century mosaic showing the loaves and fishes of Jesus's miracle – the feeding of the multitude. It is in the Church of the Multiplying of the Loaves, Tabgha, Israel.

Published by Warwick Press, 730 Fifth Avenue, New York, New York, 10019.

First published in Great Britain by Longman Group Limited in 1981.

Copyright © 1981 Grisewood & Dempsey Ltd.

Printed in Italy by Vallardi Industrie Grafiche.

6 5 4 3 2 1   All rights reserved.

Library of Congress Catalog Card No. 81-51291

ISBN 0-531-09186-4

Cover and endpapers by
Sonia Halliday Photos

Contents

Author
Theodore Rowland-Entwistle

Editor
Adrian Sington

Adviser
Professor John Ferguson, M.A., B.D., F.I.A.L.

Maps by
Tony Payne

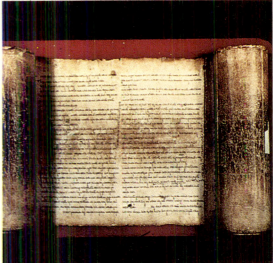

Above: The Isaiah scroll found at Qumran (left) is made of 17 pieces of leather sewn together and measures 7.5 m (24.5 ft) in length. It is thought to date from about 100 BC. Portions of over 100 scrolls of Old Testament books have been found in the caves as well as many coins dating from the reign of John Hyrcanus (135-104 BC).

Left: The caves at Qumran on the shores of the Dead Sea, where the Dead Sea Scrolls of an Essene sect were found.

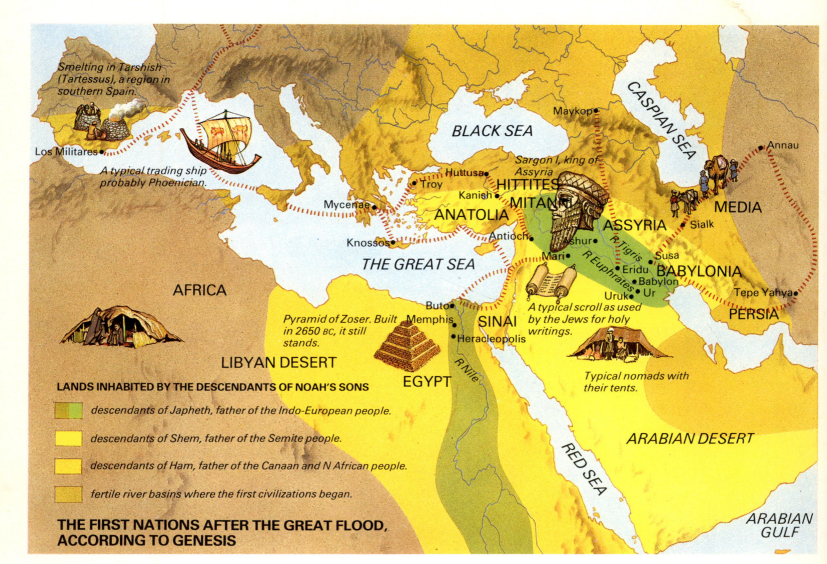

Smelting in Tarshish (Tartessus), a region in southern Spain.

Los Militares

A typical trading ship probably Phoenician.

BLACK SEA

Maykop

CASPIAN SEA

Annau

Sargon I, king of Assyria

Huttusa

Troy

Kanish

HITTITES

MITANNI

MEDIA

Mycenae

ANATOLIA

ASSYRIA

Sialk

Knossos

Antioch

Ashur

R. Tigris

Susa

Mari

R. Euphrates

Eridu

Susa

BABYLONIA

THE GREAT SEA

A typical scroll as used by the Jews for holy writings.

Babylon

Uruk

Ur

Tepe Yahya

AFRICA

Buto

PERSIA

Pyramid of Zoser. Built in 2650 BC, it still stands.

Memphis

SINAI

Heracleopolis

Typical nomads with their tents.

LIBYAN DESERT

R. Nile

EGYPT

ARABIAN DESERT

LANDS INHABITED BY THE DESCENDANTS OF NOAH'S SONS

descendants of Japheth, father of the Indo-European people.

descendants of Shem, father of the Semite people.

descendants of Ham, father of the Canaan and N African people.

fertile river basins where the first civilizations began.

RED SEA

ARABIAN GULF

THE FIRST NATIONS AFTER THE GREAT FLOOD, ACCORDING TO GENESIS

The ancient world as it was during most of Biblical history. The known world was centered on the Mediterranean Sea and the lands immediately to the east of it – the modern Middle East. The Jews originated in Mesopotamia, the land between the Tigris and Euphrates rivers in what is now Iraq. The lines marked with dashes show the main trading routes.

The Ancient World

Genesis 6-9

A large part of the Bible is devoted to the story of the Jewish people – their origins, their travels, their wars, their defeats and triumphs. For this reason, the area of the Bible lands ranges much farther than modern Israel and Jordan. It covers the whole of what is today generally called the Middle East. It ranges from Egypt in the west to Iran, then called Persia, in the east, and from Anatolia (the Asian part of Turkey) in the north to the edge of the Arabian desert in the south. In addition the New Testament takes the story into Greece, the Central Mediterranean and Italy.

First Civilizations

In the heart of this region lay Babylonia and Assyria, which occupied most of what is now known as Iraq. Here, in Mesopotamia, the region "between" and around the two great rivers of the area, the Tigris and the Euphrates, developed one of the world's earliest civilizations. What is now Iran was the land of the Medes (in the north) and the

Persians (farther south). The Hittites, who appear in the Bible narrative, occupied Anatolia. Canaan, the Promised Land of the Jewish people, was what is now Israel and western Jordan, Lebanon and the coastal part of modern Syria. The word Canaan meant "the land of purple", and it was so called because the people who lived there made a purple dye from shellfish which they caught in the Mediterranean Sea. From the Latin name of one species of shellfish, *Purpura*, comes the English word purple. The Canaanites, who settled along the coastal strip in the northwest of Palestine, were great travelers, traders and colonizers. They are better known in history under their other name, Phoenicians, the name given them by the Greeks.

The Written Account

The Bible is a collection of books which is divided into two parts. The Old Testament is concerned with Jewish traditions and history, while the New Testament tells the story of Jesus and the origins of Christianity. The Old Testament is a mixture of history, legend, poetry, prophecy and Jewish religious law.

Today, thanks to the discoveries of archaeologists and their diggings in the ruins of ancient cities, we have evidence to check the history of the Jewish people, as told in the Bible. It began in about 1900 BC, and continued until the Jewish people were scattered, which is known as the *Diaspora* (dispersion) and the destruction of Jerusalem in AD 70.

Power of the Myth

For a long time the record of the past, whether Jewish or non-Jewish, was not written down. It was passed on from one generation to the next by word of mouth. We are beginning to realize, in studying African history, for example, that oral tradition may preserve historical fact, though often in an embroidered form. In addition we must remember the importance of myth. Myth is not fiction. Myth may be based on historical events. However, what matters in myth is not historical accuracy but the imaginative or spiritual message.

An example is the story of the Flood, which is told in *Genesis 6-9*. As told in the Bible, God decided to destroy the human race because of its wickedness, but he preserved one man who led a pure life, Noah and his family. He commanded Noah to build a great boat, the Ark, into which Noah took his family and specimens of every living animal. God then sent a flood which covered the whole Earth, killing everybody.

Similar legends about a great flood are widely found. The Greeks had one. In Mesopotamia (from which tradition had it that Abraham migrated) there is a similar story, *The Epic of Gilgamesh*.

The Archaeologists

Archaelogists digging in the ruins of Babylonia have found traces of several disastrous floods. In about 4000 BC, one of them overwhelmed Ur, the city from which Abraham came. It covered everything with a layer of fine clay about 3 meters (10 feet) thick. This appears to have been the greatest of many floods, some of which happened more than a thousand years later. To people who did not travel much, and whose knowledge of the lands around them was limited, a flood of this kind would seem as though it covered the whole world.

During the past hundred years, archaeologists have made many important discoveries in the Bible lands, which have helped to bring to life the Bible stories. The tablets and inscriptions of the Babylonians and Assyrians refer to many people and events in Jewish history, and sculptures and wall-paintings there and in Egypt also relate to biblical events. The ruins of cities long forgotten have been found buried under mounds of rubbish. Carvings in these ruins show what the people mentioned in the Bible looked like – Hittites with their pronounced features, the fierce Assyrian kings, the noble Persian warriors. Again, the ruins of Greek and Roman settlements have provided valuable clues to the events of the New Testament, including the pavement on which Jesus stood while Pilate sat in judgment of him.

Above: This view of the Judean desert west of Jericho gives some idea of the bleakness of the wilderness lands through which Abraham and his family traveled on their way to Canaan. Only a few isolated plants grow in the desert landscape.

Below: By contrast, many parts of the ancient Middle East were rich, fertile lands. They were cultivated by primitive means, such as this ox-drawn beam used for breaking up the soil. Canaan was very fertile and was described as "a land of milk and honey".

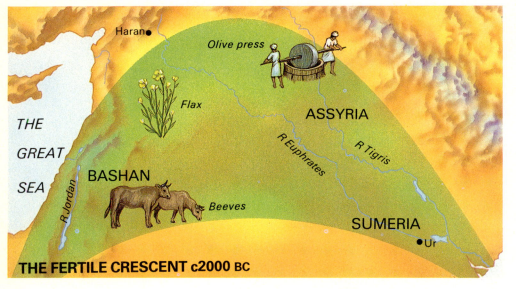

THE FERTILE CRESCENT c2000 BC

The Fertile Crescent as it appeared at the time of Abraham. Ur, Abraham's native city, was part of the land of Sumer in the southeast. The inset pictures show flax, the principal plant from which fabrics were made; the small native cattle of Palestine; and olives being crushed in a simple mill to extract the oil.

Ur of the Chaldees

Genesis 10

The Bible tells us that Abraham, the ancestor of the Israelites, came originally from Ur of the Chaldees. Ur was a city in what is now southern Iraq, lying close to the Euphrates river. Today the ruins of Ur lie in the midst of an expanse of gray mud and yellow sand, broken by occasional mounds under which lie the remains of more lost cites. It is hard to realize that this was once a green and fertile land, with waving fields of wheat and flourishing palm trees. There is still some vegetation close to the Euphrates, but where the irrigation canals bringing water to the fields stop, the crops cannot grow so they stop too, as if marked off by a ruler.

The dramatic change in Ur came about some time around 300 BC, when the Euphrates silted up and changed its course. The river now flows about 16 km (10 miles) from the site of Ur. When the river bed changed its position all the elaborate systems of irrigation became useless.

Building Houses

Ur was first settled some time before 4000 BC, but the early settlement was wiped out by a great flood. Before that time there were wide marshes close to the Euphrates, but they had started to dry up. After the flood new settlers arrived. These people came from the north. They were metalworkers, using bronze, gold and silver. Ur became a rich and mighty city. Most of its buildings were constructed of mud bricks, baked rock-hard in the hot sunshine. The earliest buildings at Ur were huts made of reeds. The framework of these huts was a series of pillars made of bundles of reeds tied together, with reed mats tied between

them. The brick buildings copied this kind of structure, with pillars connected by shallower panels.

Ur was a city state of Sumeria, which was the birthplace of one of the world's oldest civilizations. It was in Sumeria that cuneiform writing developed. The word cuneiform means wedge-shaped, and scholars gave this writing the name because it was made by wedge-shaped incisions on clay tablets.

Abraham lived in Ur in about 1900 BC at a time of transition. Ur had been capital of a mighty empire which stretched from the Gulf northwards to Assyria, under the rule of kings descended from Ur-Nammu. Ur-Nammu probably reigned in the 2000s BC, and introduced a code of laws which is the oldest known. But by Abraham's time the Empire of Ur was crumbling, giving way to the first Dynasty of Babylon. The result was a large influx of foreigners into the empire's capital – Ur. This makes the question of Abraham's racial origins and therefore the origin of the Hebrew race complicated.

Origin of the Hebrews

The language spoken by Abraham is thought to have been a Semitic or Western Asian tongue, known as Akkadian. It was first spoken by tribes living about 400 kms (250 miles) up the Euphrates river valley. Semitic languages are closely related and, because most of the languages spoken throughout the Fertile Crescent were Semitic, Abraham would have had little trouble conversing with strangers when he left Ur on his travels. The traveling party included Abraham's wife, Sarai and his nephew, Lot.

They moved northwards along a trade route which was old even in Abraham's day. It leads from the Euphrates to the seaports on the Mediterranean Sea coast. Abraham's popularity increased, and it seems that most of his early followers who were to be called the Hebrews, lived around Haran in Aramea. Today it lies in southern Turkey.

The Aramean Hebrews seem to have been shepherds on the desert edge of the Fertile Crescent, and though the Arameans contributed only a small part of the ultimately very mixed blood of the Israelites, the earliest traditions are Aramean. Later Abraham always regarded Haran as his "home town".

What sort of life was Abraham leaving behind? According to the Bible he was a prosperous man, so he probably lived in the main residential quarter of Ur. There, archaeologists have found the ruins of well-built, spacious family houses, with plenty of room not only for a large family but also for servants. Each house had its own area used for family worship.

The city contained many fine buildings, the most important of which was a ziggurat, a vast brick structure like a stepped pyramid. On top was a shrine dedicated to the Moon-god, Nanna or Sin, which the pagan people of Ur worshiped. The city was a bustling trade center with links by sea – through ports farther down the Gulf – with India and eastern Asia. From the East came the gold and silver which have been found in such profusion in the graves of the kings of Ur. These graves occupied a large open site outside the city walls, but not far from the ziggurat and the shrine of the Moon-god. Sixteen royal graves have been found there and hundreds of other graves as well. The dead kings and queens were surrounded, not only by objects which the dead might be supposed to need in their afterlife, but also by the bodies of their attendants, who were slain or took their lives so they could accompany their royal masters and mistresses into the next life. The Bible says that it may have been traditions of that kind and the pagan religious worship which led Abraham to leave Ur.

Lifespans

One problem for scholars trying to decide exactly when Abraham lived is his extraordinarily long life, which was 175 years according to the Bible story. The Bible says that his father lived even longer, dying at 205. It is possible that there was more than one Abraham, and that accounts for the two have become confused. It is notable that the more shadowy figures in the Bible stories have the longest lives – Noah, for instance, is credited with 950 years – and that the closer we come to the time when Bible stories were written down, the more ordinary the lifespans become.

CUNEIFORM WRITING

Cuneiform was a system of writing invented by the Sumerians around 3000 BC. The name means "wedge-shaped", and scholars chose it because the writing was made by impressing the letters into clay tablets with a stylus which had a three-sided tip. It was used widely in the Middle East from before the time of Abraham almost until the time of Jesus. Thousands of clay tablets from royal libraries have been found, some of which provide additional evidence for some of the Bible stories.

Above: The modern village of Haran, in southern Turkey, the site of the city where Abraham settled for a time. The few hundred people who now live there occupy these unusual mud-brick houses, built like an old-fashioned beehive in shape.

Left: The ziggurat at Ur, probably the best preserved of the 25 ziggurats known in the Middle East. Ziggurats were temple towers stepped, roughly in the shape of a pyramid. The most famous was at Babylon, the Tower of Babel, referred to in Genesis 11. The ziggurat at Ur was built by the Sumerians, the first occupiers of the city, around 2100 BC. The Bible calls the city "Ur of the Chaldees".

Travels of Abraham

Genesis 11-15

The semi-desert shores of the Dead Sea, with a few scattered trees and some small, scrubby shrubs. In the background, to the east, lie the hills of Moab, which now form part of Jordan. According to the Bible narrative Moab was named after Lot's grandson, who settled there with his family. Inset: Bedouin children guide a flock of sheep and goats across the Judean desert near Jericho. In just such a way Abraham and his flocks traveled through the land, nearly four thousand years ago. Wandering tribes move their animals from one grazing ground to another, moving on as soon as the scanty supply of vegetation has been eaten.

After spending some time in the northern city of Haran, Abraham's father Terah, died. So Abraham was called by God to go west in search of new lands. "Now the Lord said unto Abraham, 'Get thee out of the country . . into a land that I will show thee: and I will make of thee a great nation, and I will bless thee and make thy name great'." (*Genesis 12:1-2.*)

Egyptian inscriptions of the time show that Canaan was a land of contrasts. The coastal strip with its seaports lay under Egyptian control, and there was a brisk trade in timber and a variety of other goods. Isolated inland towns were connected by trade roads. They were subject to raids by parties of wandering Bedouins and other nomads who the Egyptians called "Sand-ramblers". An account of life in Canaan was written by an Egyptian nobleman named Sinuhe, who fled there to escape from his political enemies in the 1900s BC. He described the country in words almost identical to those used in the Bible (*Deuteronomy 8*), when Moses was planning his departure from Egypt.

The first place Abraham and his party reached was the sanctuary of Shechem. Its ruins were found in 1914, not far from a

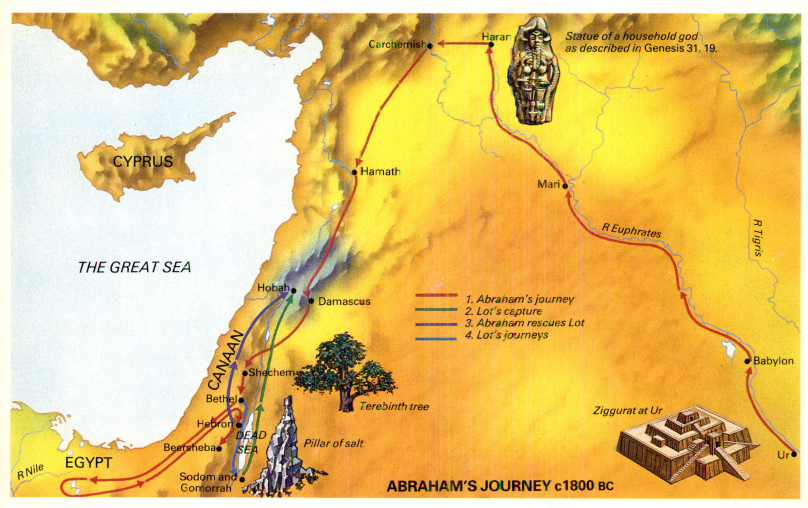

Carchemish · · Haran

Statue of a household god as described in Genesis 31, 19.

CYPRUS

THE GREAT SEA

· Hamath

Mari

R Euphrates

R Tigris

Hobah · Damascus

1. Abraham's journey
2. Lot's capture
3. Abraham rescues Lot
4. Lot's journeys

CANAAN

· Shechem

Babylon

Bethel ·

Terebinth tree

Hebron ·

DEAD SEA

Pillar of salt

Ziggurat at Ur

Beersheba ·

R Nile   EGYPT

Sodom and Gomorrah ·

ABRAHAM'S JOURNEY c1800 BC

Ur ·

small village in Jordan called Ashkar. Shechem and many other small towns that have been found since were heavily fortified strongholds, places of refuge where people could take shelter in time of danger.

Egypt

When Abraham arrived in Canaan there was famine, so he and his party continued on their way to Egypt. That country, with regular flooding from the Nile, had an excellent record of crop production. In later times it supplied shiploads of grain to Rome. Wall paintings found in the tomb of an Egyptian nobleman at Beni-Hasan, 320 kilometres (200 miles) south of Cairo, show a group of people described in an inscription as "Sand-dwellers". This may refer to Abraham's people. Their appearance and dress is just what we should expect from reading biblical descriptions of clothing. The men have long, dark hair, neat beards and knee-length sleeveless cloaks.

On their return to Canaan, Abraham and Lot found they had such huge herds of cattle that they had to split up to find adequate grazing.

Abraham settled at Hebron. He built an altar close to a grove of terebinth trees, and there he eventually died. For hundreds of years the Arabs of Palestine have called a site near Hebron "the sanctuary on the hill of Abraham". Archaeologists have found there, traces of a very ancient altar and the roots of mighty long-dead trees close to it. There is also a well, which would have been needed at a settlement.

Sodom and Gomorrah

Lot settled in the well-watered lands of the River Jordan valley, making his base in the Vale of Siddim, south of the Dead Sea. The Dead Sea is one of the most remarkable places on Earth. Its surface is in a deep cleft in the land, 396 meters (1300 feet) below the level of the Mediterranean Sea, and the water is 25 per cent solid salt.

In the Vale of Siddim were two cities – most likely small settlements – called Sodom and Gomorrah. The Bible tells a gruesome story of the wickedness of the people that lived there, and how the Lord destroyed the cities with "fire and brimstone from the skies". There is now no trace of Sodom, Gomorrah or the Vale of Siddim. But at the southern end of the Dead Sea is a shallow area, partly cut off from the rest by the peninsula of el-Lisan. Traces of tree stumps have been sighted under the water here, and it seems likely that this was the Vale of Siddim. The Dead Sea lies in a huge fault in the Earth's surface, an area of earthquakes and volcanic activity. It is most probable that there was an earthquake in which Sodom and Gomorrah were destroyed and the Vale of Siddim sank to be covered by the salt waters.

Lot and his family fled to safety, but his wife, according to the Bible, was turned into a pillar of salt. There are many salt encrusted rock pillars in the tortured landscape near the Dead Sea, one of which may well have seemed human in appearance to the terrified refugees, searching for a missing member of their party.

The journeys of Abraham, from his native city, Ur, to Haran; from Haran to Canaan; and from Canaan to Egypt and back. These journeys are marked on the key. Route 2 shows that taken by the four kings, of Elam, Goyim, Shinar and Ellasar, when they took Abraham's nephew Lot away as a prisoner to Hobah. Route 3 shows how Abraham set out from Hebron to rescue Lot. Route 4 is the original route taken by Lot when he and Abraham decided to part company. The story is told in Genesis 13 and 14.

Into Egypt

Genesis 16-end

Abraham had many descendants. The Bible tells us of his first son, Ishmael, by his wife's maid named Hagar. She was an Egyptian slave-girl. Then his wife Sarai, by now called Sarah, had a son, at a time when she was supposed to be too old for child-bearing. Sarah's son was Isaac. There was also an unspecified number of sons by other wives. It was quite normal in those times for a man who could afford it to have more than one wife.

Isaac had two sons, twins named Esau and Jacob. Although Esau was the elder son, it was Jacob who was favored, and the Bible story concentrates on the activities of Jacob and his descendants. Jacob had twelve sons, by four wives: Reuben, Simeon, Levi, Judah, Issachar, Zebulun, Joseph, Benjamin, Dan, Naphtali, Gad and Asher. Joseph and Benjamin were Jacob's sons by his favorite wife, Rachel, and Benjamin was the youngest of all.

Jacob's name was changed to Israel, meaning "who struggles with God", after a strange episode when he wrestled all night with a mysterious being. Jacob's descendants have been known as Israelites ever since. The modern state of Israel takes its name from the same source. Abraham, Isaac and Jacob are together referred to as "the Patriarchs", the "founding fathers" of the Israelites.

Joseph

The Bible continues with the story of Joseph, the favorite and second youngest son of Jacob. His father's love for him, and Joseph's own attitude to his brothers made them loathe him. He gave bad reports of them to their father. The brothers threw him into a pit to die, but instead he was found and sold as a slave to a passing caravan of traders on their way to Egypt traveling by camel.

When the caravan reached Egypt the traders sold Joseph as a slave to an Egyptian official named Potiphar, described in the Bible as the captain of the guard. Joseph became Potiphar's personal servant, but upset Potiphar's wife. As a result he was thrown into prison. A very similar story was found written on a papyrus scroll (the Egyptian equivalent of paper), which was made many hundreds of years later.

Strangely, it is the only real clue to the presence of Joseph in Egypt. For at that time Egypt had come under the rule of foreign invaders from the north. The invaders were warlike people who rode into battle in chariots, which the Egyptian soldiers did not use. These invaders arrived about 1730 BC and made themselves

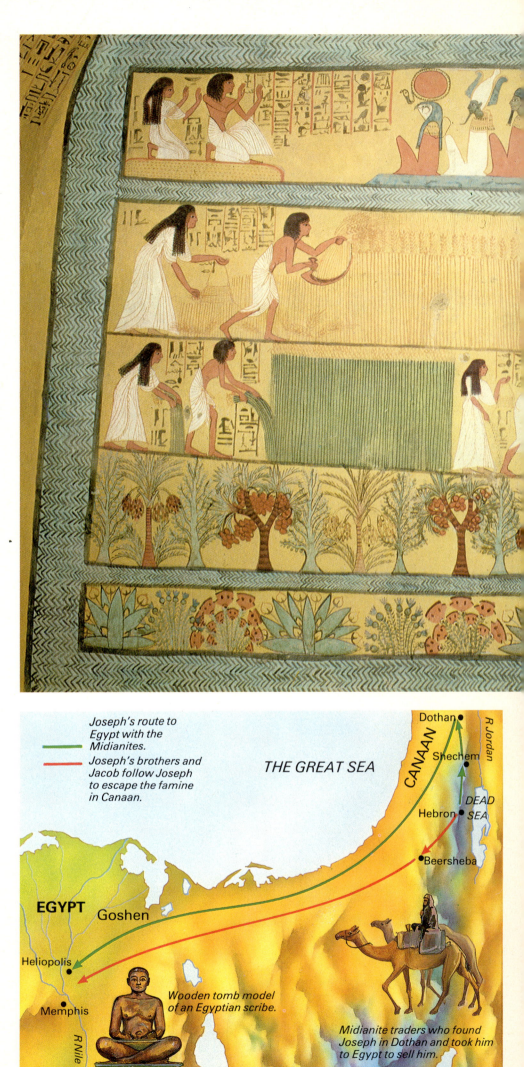

Joseph's route to Egypt with the Midianites.

Joseph's brothers and Jacob follow Joseph to escape the famine in Canaan.

THE GREAT SEA

CANAAN

Dothan

Shechem

R Jordan

DEAD SEA

Hebron

Beersheba

EGYPT

Goshen

Heliopolis

Memphis

R Nile

Wooden tomb model of an Egyptian scribe.

Midianite traders who found Joseph in Dothan and took him to Egypt to sell him.

SINAI

TRAVELS OF JOSEPH AND HIS FAMILY c1750 BC

Above: From the 1200 BC tomb, near Luxor, of an Egyptian nobleman named Sennedem comes this vivid wall-painting showing how Egyptian farmers worked.

Below: A modern Bedouin with his camel and his tent in Israel. Tribes have traveled and camped in this way since early Biblical times.

Abraham's family, the Founders of the Jewish Faith

```
                    ABRAHAM – SARAH
REUBEN ┐            ISAAC – REBECCA
SIMEON │
LEVI   │        ESAU        JACOB ┐
JUDAH  │            ── sons of Leah ──
ISSACHAR │          ── sons of Rachel ──
ZEBULUN ┘
JOSEPH ┐           ── sons of Leah's maid, Zilpah──
BENJAMIN ┘         ── sons of Rachel's maid, Bilhah──
GAD ┐
ASHER ┘
NAPHTALI ┐
DAN      ┘
```

The sons of Jacob founded the 12 tribes of Israel

Left: The Midianites, a group of tribespeople, lived in northwestern Arabia. The Egyptian scribes were people who could read and write. They served as clerks, letter-writers and civil servants. The term "scribe" as used in the Bible usually means a "man wise in the law".

pharaohs or kings of Egypt. Up to that time the Egyptians kept a careful record, either in carved inscriptions or in papyrus scrolls, of events as they occurred. From 1730 BC onwards, until 1580 BC, a period of 150 years, there are no accounts of events in Egypt. So there are no Egyptian records of the presence of Joseph and other Israelites in Egypt.

Some mention of Joseph might have been expected, too, because the Bible tells us that he rose to be viceroy of Egypt, under the pharaoh of the day. The biblical description of his appointment, receiving a ring, fine linen robe and a gold chain, is exactly like the ceremony of installing a viceroy as shown in Egyptian wall pictures. The Bible explains that Joseph won Pharaoh's good opinion by explaining a dream that he had. His explanation was that there would be seven years of good crops followed by seven years of famine. As viceroy, Joseph prepared for the famine by storing grain during the good years.

The Hyksos

Under normal Egyptian rule no "Sand-rambler" would have been allowed to rise to power. But the foreign rulers of Egypt did not despise wandering tribes who herded sheep and goats, as the Egyptians despised them. They appear to have come from the same part of the world, Canaan, and they may have been Phoenicians. According to a history of Egypt written by Manetho, an Egyptian priest of the 200s BC, they were Hyksos, "Shepherd kings", and the Jewish historian Flavius Josephus, who died about AD 100, even identifies them with the Israelites.

Despite the lack of official histories, there are a number of other clues to the presence of Israelites in Egypt at this time. The fortress of Avaris, in the Nile delta, stands on a mound called *Tell el Yahudiyeh*, "the Mound of the Jew", and Manetho says it was built by the Hyksos. Joseph rode in a chariot, says the Bible, and chariots were introduced into Egypt by the Hyksos. There are also the ruins of many grain stores to be found in Egypt, for famine was not unknown in that country.

As the famine which struck Egypt also hit Canaan, Joseph's brothers and father joined him in Egypt, where there was still food to be had. With their families they formed a party more than 70 strong. They settled in an area called Goshen in the Bible. Goshen was apparently the region on the east bank of the Nile delta, covering part of the present line of the Suez Canal, and it had grazing land for the Israelites' animals. In due course Jacob and Joseph both died and their bodies were embalmed, an Egyptian custom for preserving corpses which was not usually carried out by the Jews. The biblical description of this tallies with normal Egyptian practice.

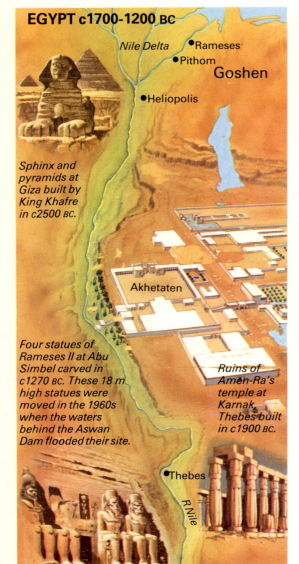

EGYPT c1700-1200 BC

Nile Delta
• Rameses
• Pithom
Goshen
• Heliopolis

Sphinx and pyramids at Giza built by King Khafre in c2500 BC.

Akhetaten

Four statues of Rameses II at Abu Simbel carved in c1270 BC. These 18 m high statues were moved in the 1960s when the waters behind the Aswan Dam flooded their site.

Ruins of Amen-Ra's temple at Karnak, Thebes built in c1900 BC.

• Thebes

R. Nile

Egypt in Biblical times. The Pyramids and the Sphinx were already old when Abraham visited the land; the city of Akheteten was built between the time of the Exodus and the Palestinian conquests of Sheshonk I. Its creator was the Pharaoh Akhenaten, the only Egyptian ruler to believe in one god – the Sun.

Events in Egypt up to the Exodus

Old Kingdom c2686-2181. 3rd-6th Dynasties. Sphinx and great pyramids built.
1st Intermediate Period c2181-2050. Disorder.
Middle Kingdom c2050-1786. 11th-14th Dynasties. Egypt is rich and powerful.
2nd Intermediate Period c1786-1567. Invasion of Hyksos from Phoenicia c1730-1580. Joseph rises to be Viceroy under the Hyksos.
New Kingdom c1567-1085. 18th-20th Dynasty. Egypt's Golden Age.
18TH DYNASTY: c1567-1320. First victimization of Israelites. Tuthmosis III completes the temple to the god, Amen-Ra at Karnak.
Akhenaten builds the city of Akhetaten to glorify the god, Aten.
Tutankamun restores the capital to Thebes, home of the god, Amen.
19TH DYNASTY: c1320-1200. The Rameses Dynasty.
Rameses I.
Seti I orders the enslavement of Israelites.
Rameses II 1292-1237. The greatest of Egyptian builders. Allows Israelites to leave Egypt.

The Years of Bondage

Exodus 1-13

The 150-year rule of the Hyksos kings in Egypt came to an end about 1580 BC. The new rulers, descendants of Sekenenre, came from Upper Egypt, much farther north. There they would have had little to do with the Israelites, and they had probably forgotten the activities of Joseph as viceroy several generations before.

The new Pharaoh noticed that the Israelites had multiplied in numbers, and he was afraid that they would in time try to take over the country, just as the Hyksos had done. So he gave instructions that all the boy babies were to be killed at birth. The orders were ignored, and the numbers of Israelites continued to rise.

Story of Moses

At this point the Bible introduces the story of Moses. He was the child of a descendant of Israel's son Levi. His mother hid him in a basket among the reeds on the banks of the Nile to prevent Moses being killed. There the baby was found by Pharaoh's daughter, who adopted him and called him Moses. This is an Egyptian name meaning "son of", and it is found as part of many Egyptian names: Rameses, for instance, is really Ra-Moses, "son of Ra", who was the Egyptian Sun-god.

The Israelites, says the Bible, now treated as slaves, were set to build two store-cities, Pithom and Rameses. These two cities were in the Nile delta, but archaeologists are not yet agreed exactly where they were. Several city sites have been found in the area, each with granaries for storing grain and store-houses for other foodstuffs. The Egyptian granaries were built very much on the lines of a modern silo, though on a smaller scale.

It is not certain which Pharaoh of Egypt ordered the enslavement of the Israelites, but it may possibly have been Seti I, who reigned 1313-1292 BC. His father was Rameses I, so the store-city could well have been named after him. Seti was a great warrior who fought several successful campaigns in Palestine and Syria.

The Bible narrative goes on to tell how Moses killed an Egyptian who was beating one of the Israelite slaves and had to flee to the Land of Midian taking his brother Aaron with him. This territory lies to the north-east of the Gulf of Aqaba. Here while pasturing flocks he had a powerful mystical experience. He saw a bush blazing without being destroyed and heard a voice pro-

A pharaoh wearing the double crown of Egypt, kilt and richly colored cloak decorated with embroidered feathers. The crook and flail are symbols of care and power which a pharaoh exercises over his people.

claiming himself the God of Abraham, Isaac and Jacob with a name usually transliterated Yahweh and meaning I AM or I AM THAT I AM.

While Moses was in exile, the Pharaoh died. It is thought that the new Pharaoh was his son, Rameses II. Rameses II was a remarkable man, though a very vain one. He spent 17 years of his long reign in wars against the Hittites, who had a powerful empire based in Anatolia (modern Turkey). Eventually Rameses made peace with the Hittites. Under the peace treaty he married a Hittite princess and secured control of Palestine – which had indeed been under Egyptian occupation for some time.

During their years of bondage in Egypt the Israelites were forced to make bricks. Although the finest buildings, such as temples, were built of stone, most of the ordinary buildings such as houses were made of brick. Bricks as we know them are baked in kilns, which need large quantities of fuel to raise the temperature to around 1000°C. But Egypt has always been short of wood, the main fuel used until comparatively recently. So most Egyptian bricks were baked hard in the fierce heat of the sun. If straw is mixed in with the mud or clay from which the bricks are made, they can be fired in heaps with just a little extra fuel to start things off. Such a method of firing produces a temperature of about 600°C, sufficient to completely harden the mud.

When Moses and his brother Aaron re-turned to Egypt and urged their fellow-Israelites to stop working so that they could worship the Lord, the Egyptians were annoyed. As a punishment they ordered the Israelites to gather their own straw for making bricks, while still keeping output at the same level. From this comes our popular saying "to make bricks without straw" – to do something without the necessary materials.

The Egyptians were understandably reluctant to let the Israelites leave their land, when Moses asked Pharaoh to free them. Slave labour is worth a lot of money. The Bible says that Pharaoh was persuaded to release the slaves following a series of plagues or disasters. The Israelites believed that God had brought these about to free them from bondage and as a punishment for the Egyptians' refusal to let them go.

The first disaster was when the waters of the Nile turned to blood. From time to time reddish soil from Ethiopia does turn the Nile red. Swarms of flies infested the houses of the Egyptians, and still do from time to time. An epidemic killed the cattle, and another one gave people boils. Finally there was a plague of locusts, and dense swarms of locusts are still a nightmare in parts of Africa and Asia. It was followed by darkness. Fearing that the God of the Israelites was causing all these troubles, the Egyptians agreed to let them depart, although they later pursued them to try to bring them back.

Making mud or clay bricks in Egypt. The method has changed very little in the past 5000 years. Each brick is formed in a mold and is then laid out in the sun to dry for a few days. Egyptian builders used a clay mortar to bond their bricks together. They were first class bricklayers. The sizes of bricks varied, and experts can use these variations to help date a building.

In the Wilderness

Exodus 14-end
Leviticus
Numbers 1-10

In the autumn quails migrate southwards from Europe to Africa, flying over the eastern Mediterranean area. To this day they alight on the shores of the Red Sea for a rest. So the Israelites were able to catch them as described in Exodus 16.

The Israelites also ate fruits such as figs, olives, pomegranates and grapes whilst in the Wilderness. Beans, lentils, cucumbers, grain and gourds could grow in the rugged ground and the nomads would eat them cooked with salt and herbs.

Milk from their goats and sheep was made into yogurt known as Leben. This can be kept indefinitely in little cloth sacks. Butter could also be made and was considered a delicacy. A tribe's hospitality was measured by the quality of its butter and was used as a means of payment.

The departure of the Israelites from Egypt, known as the Exodus, has set archaeologists and other scholars some of the Bible's hardest problems. We know they began by going south. The main route to Canaan was to the north, along the Mediterranean Sea coastline, as it still is. But the Pharaoh's soldiers would be guarding that route, so Moses led his people in the opposite direction. They camped on the shores of the sea – but which sea? The Hebrew words *Yam Suph* can be variously translated as Red Sea or Reed Sea, and either is possible.

Before the Suez Canal was built in the 1860s there was a sea of reeds now absorbed in the canal. The last named stopping place of the Israelites, Migdol, lies about 24 kilometers (15 miles) north of present-day Suez, very close to the Gulf of Suez which is the northwest arm of the Red Sea. When the Israelites came to cross the sea they were hotly pursued by the Egyptian cavalry and charioteers.

The Bible tells how God sent a strong wind to blow back the waters of the sea, so that the refugees could cross dry-shod. After the Israelites had crossed, the wind dropped, the waters returned and the pursuing Egyptians were drowned. The Israelites, with their flocks, were safe in the wilderness of the Sinai Peninsula. The deliverance from Egypt was an event which etched itself on the memory of the Israelites. They attributed it to God, Yahweh. Time and again the prophets speak in His name: "I am the Lord your God, who brought you out of the land of Egypt".

Living in the Wilderness

The popular term wilderness, like desert, can be misleading. Sinai is both a wilderness and a desert, but people can and do live there. There is not much rain each year, but usually there is enough for a few plants to grow – enough to provide grazing for wandering flocks of sheep and goats. This is typical of a great part of the Middle East.

The Israelites came into this region of scanty plant life from a land where food was plentiful. Not surprisingly, they complained bitterly. But the desert yielded unexpected sources of food, which the Bible describes in picturesque terms. There was a flock of quails, which could be caught and killed for food. To this day quails appear in Sinai every year, during their autumn migration from Europe to the south. This gives us a

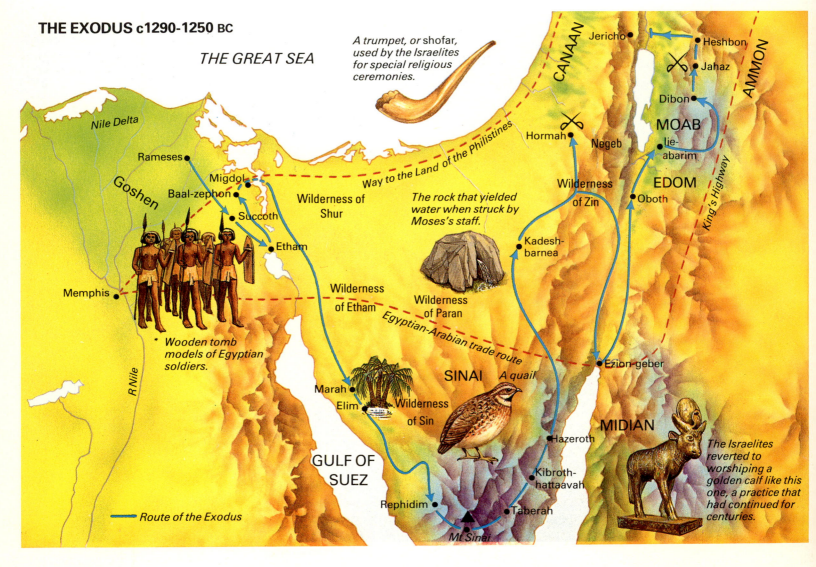

THE EXODUS c1290-1250 BC

THE GREAT SEA

A trumpet, or shofar, used by the Israelites for special religious ceremonies.

Nile Delta

Rameses
Migdol
Baal-zephon
Succoth
Goshen
Memphis
Etham

Wooden tomb models of Egyptian soldiers.

R Nile

Wilderness of Shur

Wilderness of Etham

The rock that yielded water when struck by Moses's staff.

Wilderness of Paran

Egyptian-Arabian trade route

Marah
Elim
Wilderness of Sin

GULF OF SUEZ

Rephidim
Mt Sinai

A quail

SINAI

Hazeroth
Kibroth-hattaavah
Taberah

MIDIAN

The Israelites reverted to worshiping a golden calf like this one, a practice that had continued for centuries.

Way to the Land of the Philistines

CANAAN

Jericho
Heshbon
Jahaz
Dibon
Hormah
Negeb
MOAB
lie-abarim
AMMON

Wilderness of Zin

EDOM
Oboth

Kadesh-barnea

King's Highway

Ezion-geber

— *Route of the Exodus*

The Arabs call it Jebel Musa – the Mount of Moses, a name preserving an old tradition. This rugged granite peak is in the southern part of the Sinai Peninsula, and is believed to be the mountain where Moses received the Ten Commandments from God. There has been a Greek monastery on Jebel Musa since AD 250.

Left: Probable route of the Exodus. The Israelites avoided the two main routes to Canaan, the coastal road and the King's Highway. Instead they took a less direct way, wandering with their flocks from one scanty wilderness pasture to another.

time of year for the Exodus from Egypt.

The greatest miracle to the Israelites was manna, fine flakes which appeared every morning, but melted when the sun grew hot. Among the few plants which grow freely there are tamarisks, small shrubby trees which can flourish in places where there is a lot of salt and very little water. Living on the tamarisk bushes is a species of plant louse, or aphid, which pierces the stems of the tamarisks to suck out the juices. Like other aphids, it produces a sweet, sticky substance, known as honeydew, on which ants feed. This honeydew is the manna of the Bible, and the wandering Bedouin tribes of the area still use it for food. The Bedouin who live there today also hunt gazelles and ibexes, which live in the Sinai Peninsula.

Number of Israelites
The Israelites spent 40 years in the wilderness altogether. How many there were of them we can only guess. According to the *Book of Numbers* (*1:45-46*) there were over 600,000 males fit for military service, which would mean perhaps three times that number of men, women and children altogether. This would be equal to half the population of modern Israel and is a most unlikely figure. At the moment Sinai supports about 6000 wandering Bedouin, and it is likely that the Israelites were about that number.

Why did the Israelites spend so long in their journey? If there were indeed only 6000 of them they were probably too weak in numbers to attack and dispossess the

people already living in Canaan, the 'Promised Land'. They needed time to gain strength and plan their campaign.

The Bible gives a very full list of the places where they stopped, and archaeologists have been able to trace many of them. For example, one of the earliest encampments was at Dophkah, a name which means a place where smelting takes place. Such a site is Serabit el-Khadem, where the ancient Egyptians used to mine copper. Another place is Rephidim, where the Amalekites, a nomadic tribe already established in Sinai, fought the Israelites. That is an oasis, now called Feiran. At this spot Moses is said to have struck a rock with his staff, and water gushed out for the people to drink. This was possible because water can become trapped in limestone rock, and if the rock is fractured correctly the water gushes out.

Mount Sinai, also called Mount Horeb, is another puzzle for scholars. Some think it was Jebel Musa (Mount Moses) in the southern part of the Sinai Peninsula. Others think it lay farther north, and several peaks have been identified with it. Wherever Mount Sinai was, it was here that a covenant was struck between Yahweh and his people, that they should be his people, and he should be their God. Associated with this covenant was the simple code of laws and morals which we call the Ten Commandments. The laws are the basis of the Jewish faith and of the Christian faith which arose from it.

Into the Promised Land

Numbers 11-end
Joshua 1-11

By the time the Israelites were ready to move north and settle in Canaan, their great leader Moses was a very old man, and indeed he died within sight of what he had described to his followers as their "Promised Land". They had spent much of their period in the wilderness at Kadesh-barnea. This place lies in the Negeb desert, which forms the southernmost part of modern Israel. Most of the Negeb in this region is a land of *wadis*, dried-up river beds which flow with water only in the rainy season of winter. The name of Kadesh-barnea lingers on in the Arabic name Ain Qedeis, a small spring near a much larger water supply.

From Kadesh-barnea Moses had sent out a reconnaissance party of twelve men, one from each of the twelve tribes which made up Israel. The tribes each claimed to be descended from one of Jacob's twelve sons, though not exactly: Levi's descendants formed a caste of priests, while Joseph's tribe was split into two, named after his sons Ephraim and Manasseh. It is possible that they were organized much on the lines of the Scottish clans, and the followers of the descendants took the tribal name.

Joshua

The spying party included Joshua, a brilliant young soldier who had already distinguished himself in fierce skirmishes with another group of desert nomads, the Amalekites. He and his colleagues reported on their return that Canaan was a land "flowing with milk and honey". In other words there was plenty of food there; in support of this they brought back a huge bunch of grapes. However, there was a problem. Canaan contained strong walled towns of Amalekites, Amorites, Canaanites, Hittites and Jebusites. There were also some very tall men, whom the spies described as giants. Joshua and Caleb, of the tribe of Judah, were all for marching in and taking possession of Canaan then and there, but their colleagues and the rest of the Israelites were frightened of the strength of Canaan and its inhabitants.

At that time Canaan was still under the rule of Egypt. But Egypt was no longer a strong power, and the longer the Israelites waited, the weaker was Egyptian rule in Canaan. The various tribes whom the spies saw there warred among themselves. The ruins of towns, houses and tombs of the period show that the people had a poorer standard of living than their ancestors. The seaports, however, were still prosperous, and traders were dealing in an important new substance: iron. The Israelite invasion came at the beginning of what historians call the Iron Age. Many of the Israelites' enemies had iron weapons. The Israelites still had bronze ones, presumably because they had not been able to devote much time to invention while on the move.

So the Israelites decided to postpone their invasion. But they were still determined to mount it eventually, and Moses decided that, instead of attacking from the south, the tribes would sweep up into what is now Jordan and attack from the east across the River Jordan. He planned to march up the main road east of the river, known as the King's Highway. But the rulers of the lands through which the road passed – Edom, Moab and Ammon – refused to let a large band of raggle-taggle wanderers pass through their territories. So the Israelites went the long way round, until they came to the land of the Amorites. There they were again refused permission to go along the King's Highway. But this time the Israelites refused to take "no" for an answer and conquered the Amorites. They followed this victory with one over the kingdom of Bashan and stood poised on the banks of the Jordan ready for the invasion. Then, as prophesied, Moses died and Joshua took over the leadership.

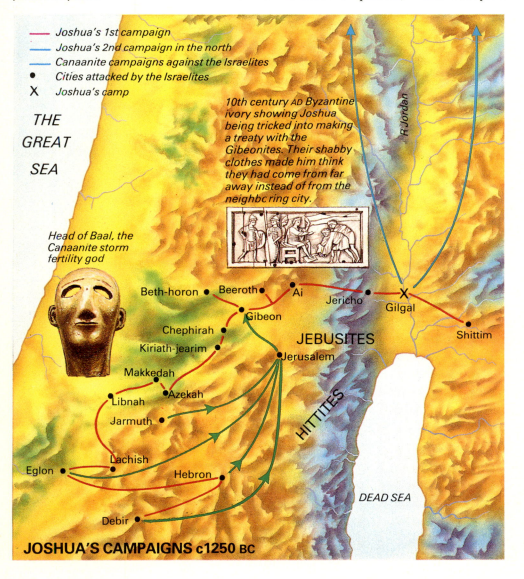

Joshua's campaigns during the conquest of Canaan. The first campaign, to the south, subdued the countryside while avoiding large, strong cities such as Jerusalem. The second campaign, to the north, also conquered the country areas but left many strongholds untouched. Later campaigns attributed to Joshua were probably carried out by local tribal leaders over a considerable period of years.

—— Joshua's 1st campaign
—— Joshua's 2nd campaign in the north
—— Canaanite campaigns against the Israelites
● Cities attacked by the Israelites
X Joshua's camp

THE GREAT SEA

10th century AD Byzantine ivory showing Joshua being tricked into making a treaty with the Gibeonites. Their shabby clothes made him think they had come from far away instead of from the neighbcring city.

Head of Baal, the Canaanite storm fertility god

Beth-horon
Beeroth
Ai
Jericho
Gilgal
Gibeon
Chephirah
Kiriath-jearim
JEBUSITES
Shittim
Makkedah
Jerusalem
Azekah
Libnah
Jarmuth
HITTITES
Lachish
Eglon
Hebron
Debir
DEAD SEA
R.Jordan

JOSHUA'S CAMPAIGNS c1250 BC

Crossing the Jordan

The invasion began with the whole band of wanderers crossing the river at a ford – and, according to the Bible, without getting their feet wet. This is quite possible, because from time to time earthquakes send tons of soil crashing into the river, creating temporary dams. The first place the Israelites came to was the walled city of Jericho, which was captured after a seven-day siege. The Bible story says that the Israelites marched round the walls seven times and when they shouted at the end of seven days, the walls fell down. Archaeologists have found that the walls of Jericho were destroyed and rebuilt, but they cannot say with certainty that they have found traces of Joshua's siege.

Joshua's army went on to capture a series of other towns. Archaeologists digging in their ruins have found evidence of fire and destruction dating from the 1200s BC; in the ruins of one, Lachish, there was a bowl bearing an inscription which has been dated at around 1230 BC. Hazor, one of the last major cities subdued by Joshua, lies about 16 kilometers (10 miles) north of the Sea of Chinnereth. Archaeologists have found evidence of its destruction in about 1200 BC.

So by 1200 BC the Israelites were in possession of a large part of Canaan. The fertile plains and some important cities such as Jerusalem remained in Canaanite control. But the Israelites could now settle in their Promised Land.

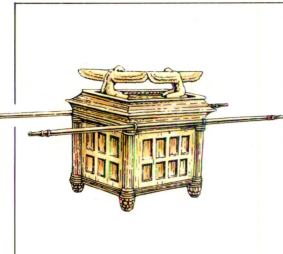

ARK OF THE COVENANT

The force which kept the Israelites together was their belief in the One God, Yahweh (Jehovah). The Ten Commandments received at Mt. Sinai were carved on stone tablets, which were kept in a wooden chest known as the Ark of the Covenant. The Ark was made of acacia wood, covered with gold, and had a solid gold lid decorated with two golden cherubim. The Ark became the most sacred possession of the Israelites, a symbol of God's presence.

BAAL

One of the problems for the religious leaders of Israel was to stop their followers from worshiping false gods. The god most frequently denounced by the Israelites was Baal, one of the supreme gods of the Canaanites. Baal was worshiped by many people in the ancient Middle East. He was a god of crops and the changing seasons and he also controlled thunder and rain. People who worshiped Baal often carried out strange rites which were disliked by the Israelite leaders. These rites sometimes included human sacrifice.

This statue of Baal was carved in the first century AD and was found at Thinissat, in Tunisia.

Trees and shrubs on the banks of the River Jordan glow in the evening sunlight. It was probably just such a peaceful sight as this which greeted the Israelites as they came down to the Jordan, ready to cross over into the Promised Land. The Bible narrative says they crossed without getting their feet wet. This may have been because the river was temporarily dammed, owing to an earthquake – something that has happened in historical times.

THE TWELVE TRIBES OF ISRAEL c1200–1020 BC

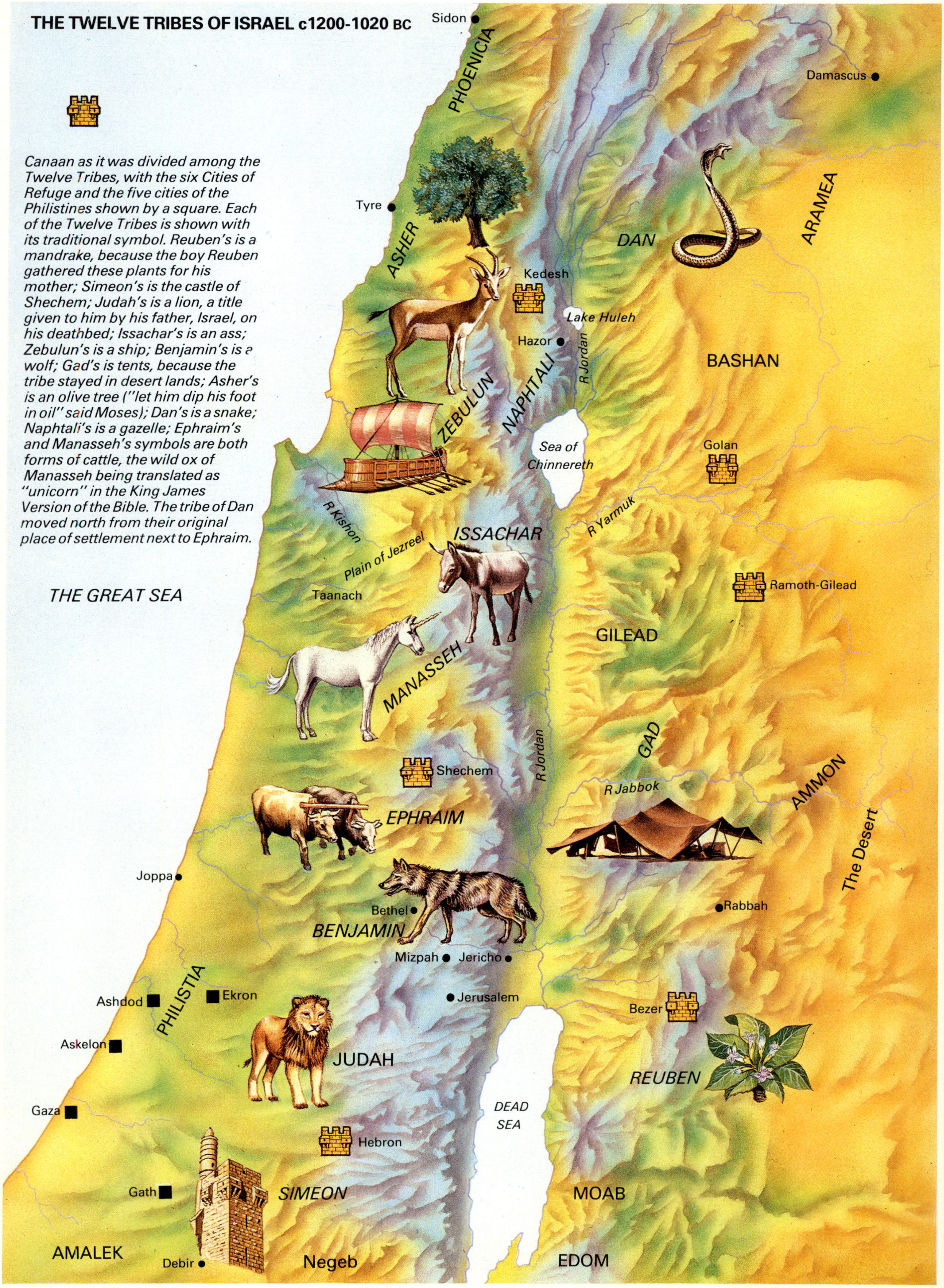

Canaan as it was divided among the Twelve Tribes, with the six Cities of Refuge and the five cities of the Philistines shown by a square. Each of the Twelve Tribes is shown with its traditional symbol. Reuben's is a mandrake, because the boy Reuben gathered these plants for his mother; Simeon's is the castle of Shechem; Judah's is a lion, a title given to him by his father, Israel, on his deathbed; Issachar's is an ass; Zebulun's is a ship; Benjamin's is a wolf; Gad's is tents, because the tribe stayed in desert lands; Asher's is an olive tree ("let him dip his foot in oil" said Moses); Dan's is a snake; Naphtali's is a gazelle; Ephraim's and Manasseh's symbols are both forms of cattle, the wild ox of Manasseh being translated as "unicorn" in the King James Version of the Bible. The tribe of Dan moved north from their original place of settlement next to Ephraim.

THE GREAT SEA

Sidon

PHOENICIA

Damascus

Tyre

ASHER

DAN

ARAMEA

Kedesh

Lake Huleh

Hazor

BASHAN

ZEBULUN

NAPHTALI

Sea of Chinnereth

Golan

R Jordan

R Kishon

Plain of Jezreel

ISSACHAR

Taanach

R Yarmuk

GILEAD

Ramoth-Gilead

MANASSEH

R Jordan

GAD

AMMON

Shechem

R Jabbok

The Desert

EPHRAIM

Joppa

Bethel

BENJAMIN

Rabbah

Mizpah   Jericho

Jerusalem

Bezer

PHILISTIA   Ekron

Ashdod

REUBEN

Askelon

JUDAH

Gaza

DEAD SEA

Hebron

Gath

SIMEON

MOAB

AMALEK

Debir   Negeb   EDOM

The Settlement

Joshua 12-end
Judges

As a rule, people do not suddenly change their ways of life. Nomads, wandering from place to place with their flocks and herds of animals, usually keep on the move. The Israelites had spent the past 40 years wandering in the wilderness, and the people already living in Canaan probably expected that these new invaders would soon go away again.

But only a generation or so back the Israelites had been living settled lives in Egypt. So it was natural that when they reached their Promised Land they immediately adopted a settled way of life again. In the ruins of the cities they had conquered they built simple houses of sun-baked mud bricks. In the mountainous regions they had conquered they started a great many small settlements, much as the colonists did in the pioneer days of America. Archaeologists have found traces of their homes in the ruins of such towns as Bethel and Debir, two of the places captured by Joshua.

Like the American pioneers, the Israelites proceeded to open up country that had not previously been occupied. In places where there were no rivers or springs to provide water, they dug cisterns deep into the stony ground and lined them with waterproof plaster. Many of these cisterns remain in good working order.

The Twelve Tribes of Israel

Joshua divided the country among the twelve tribes, as you can see in the map. The southern part of the coastline was held by the Philistines, the northern part by the Phoenicians. After many years the Israelites pushed through to the sea.

At this time Israel was not a united nation. Each of the tribes ruled itself, and indeed towns and even villages were largely self-governing. From time to time, however, an outstanding leader appeared. In the Bible these leaders are called "Judges" and they acted as local kings. The Israelites were in constant danger of war with the remaining Canaanites, and with the other tribes, such as the Moabites, Ammonites and Aramites, who were likely to raid them from the east. They fought a series of battles to preserve their independence. One of the most famous took place in the territory by the Sea of Chinnereth. There the Canaanites of the plains, who had iron chariots, held their ground against the Israelites. The Israelites were finally roused to revolt by a woman judge, the prophetess Deborah. With her help a warrior named

Barak, from the tribe of Issachar, raised an army and routed the Canaanites at Taanach in the Plain of Jezreel. The ruins of Taanach have been found, and archaeologists have found evidence of burning in one area from about 1125 BC.

A much bigger threat came from the Philistines, who occupied the coastal strip from Joppa (present-day Tel-Aviv) south to Gaza and the Negeb desert. Ruins of the Philistine coastal cities of Ashdod, Askelon and Gaza have been excavated by archaeologists, while Egyptian inscriptions record the fighting between Rameses III and the Philistines in the 1100s BC. The Philistines made a special kind of pottery, large quantities of which have been found. It was very like the pottery from Mycenae, an ancient Greek city which used to export pottery all over the Middle East until Mycenae was destroyed by invaders shortly before 1200 BC. Many of the Philistine pots were beer mugs, and the people seem to have been great beer drinkers.

During the 1100s BC the Philistines began invading the Israelite territory to the east of the coastal strip. They were resisted by a guerrilla leader named Samson, who was one of the last judges. He was a man of great physical strength. Eventually, with the help of a woman named Delilah, the Philistines captured Samson, blinded him and took him as a prisoner to Gaza. One day a group of them took him into a temple to show off his strength. Samson did so by pulling over two pillars of the temple, bringing down the roof and killing his enemies. Ruins of a temple which had two wooden pillars which a very large man might possibly reach and push over have been found at Gaza.

But exploits like this did not end the Philistine menace. As the Bible says (*Judges 21:25*) "In those days there was no king in Israel and every man did what was right in his own eyes". What the Israelites badly needed was a strong leader, and they were soon to get one.

An example of the beautifully made and decorated pottery which the Philistines produced. It is distinguished by geometrical designs, in red and black, and by stylized pictures of swans. Pottery of this kind has been found in the ruins of the five Philistine cities referred to in 1 Samuel 6:17 – Ashdod, Gaza, Askelon, Gath and Ekron.

Judges of Israel who ruled from c1200-1020 BC
Othniel of Judah
Ehud of Benjamin
Barak and Deborah
Gideon of Manasseh
Abimelech of Manasseh
Tola of Issachar
Jair of Gilead
Jephthah of Gilead
Ibzan of Bethlehem
Elon of Zebulun
Abdon of Ephraim
Samson of Dan
Samuel of Ephraim

The fertile soil of Canaan, after the bleakness of the wilderness, made it seem truly a "land flowing with milk and honey" for the Israelites who moved in to conquer it. This picture shows a group of Arabs plowing the land and sowing seed, near the modern city of Bethlehem. The Church of the Nativity in the city is over a cave where, according to local tradition, Mary gave birth to Jesus.

The Kingdom of Israel

I Samuel
II Samuel
I Kings 1-11
I Chronicles 10-end
II Chronicles 1-9

The strength of the Philistines increased after the death of Samson, and around about 1050 BC the fortunes of the Israelites reached a low point. For one thing, the Philistines had the secret of working in iron. As a result, they had iron swords, while the Israelites probably still had to make do with bronze weapons.

About this time the Philistines marched an army into Israelite territory. At a place called Eben-ezer, on the edge of the mountains at a spot which has not yet been precisely identified, a fierce battle took place and the Israelites were routed. In an effort to rally their soldiers and urge them to fight harder, the Israelite leaders sent for the Ark of the Covenant which was kept in the holy city of Shiloh – which lay about 25 kilometers (16 miles) north of modern Jerusalem. Even the presence of this, the most sacred object of Israel, was not enough to boost the army's morale. There was a second battle, and the Israelites were defeated again by a much larger army of Philistines. The Ark of the Covenant was captured. Excavations at Seilun, the modern name for the site of Shiloh, show that the city was destroyed in about 1050 BC, which suggests that the Philistines left no stone unturned in their quest to destroy the Israelite army.

According to the Bible, the Philistines sent the Ark of the Covenant back after only seven months. Their capture of it coincided with a plague of rats and an outbreak of tumors, and the Philistines thought the Ark must be the cause.

Samuel and Saul

Shortly before the death of Samson, the last Judge had arisen in Israel. He was Samuel, a peasant's son, who served as a priest in the shrine at Shiloh. He was also a prophet, and people used to come from far and wide to consult him. About 20 years after the Philistines had won the battle at Eben-ezer, Samuel commanded an Israelite army which heavily defeated yet another large army of Philistine invaders.

A few years later the tribal leaders of Israel realized that the nation needed one strong, central leader – a king. They repeatedly asked Samuel to choose one for them. He was reluctant; they should have no

Above: King Hezekiah's tunnel, which runs through solid rock for 533 m (1750 ft) under Jerusalem. It was made in 701 BC to carry the water from the spring of Gihon into the pool of Siloam, inside the city walls. Hezekiah had it dug in anticipation of an Assyrian siege of the city, in order to safeguard his water supply. Two gangs of workmen cut their way through from opposite ends. An inscription found on the wall tells how the two gangs met.

Left: Solomon's Pools, now in Israel south of Bethlehem. Although these pools may well have been constructed at the time of Solomon, there is a strong tendency to associate ancient structures with the greatest of the kings of Israel. An example is King Solomon's Mines at Timna near the Gulf of Aqaba. Although these copper mines have been worked from time to time for the past 6000 years, archaeologists are positive that they were not in use in Solomon's day.

king but Yahweh. In the end he gave way. His choice fell on Saul, the handsome son of an important family of the small tribe of Benjamin, who lived at Gibeah, a little way north of Jerusalem. At the time he became king he was probably about 50 years old, and he had a grown-up son, Jonathan.

About a month after he was anointed king by Samuel, Saul heard that the Ammonites were attacking Jabesh-Gilead, which probably lay on the east bank of the Jordan about 30 kilometers (20 miles) south of the Sea of Chinnereth. He quickly raised an army and crushed the Ammonites in a surprise dawn attack. The victory won him the support of the Israelites. Saul, using Gibeah as a base, drove the Philistines out of the Israelites' lands.

The Bible describes one skirmish at Michmash in which Saul's son Jonathan surprised the enemy at a mountain pass between two sharp-pointed rocks. (1 Samuel 14.) During the First World War (1914-1918) a British officer fighting the Turks in Palestine remembered this story when he found himself at Michmash. He repeated the surprise tactics with equal success.

David

Meanwhile David, a shepherd, had won Saul's attention by challenging and killing a huge Philistine, Goliath. But his later success as a soldier made Saul jealous of him, and David had to flee in exile. For some time he headed an outlaw band in the mountains of Engedi, near the Dead Sea. Then Saul tried to capture him, and so David and his men entered the service of Achish, the Philistine king of Gath.

When David heard of Saul's defeat and death at Mount Gilboa, he returned to the Israelite territory of Judah, where the people accepted him as their king. The northern part of the Israelite territory took Ishbosheth, another of Saul's sons, as their king. For more than seven years, civil war raged between the two factions. Then two of Ishbosheth's officers assassinated him, and the two kingdoms were united under David's rule. David had the killers put to death. He then captured the centrally placed city of Jerusalem, which was called Jebus by the Canaanite tribe that still held Jerusalem and made it the capital of his new country.

Altogether, David was king for 40 years. In that time he made the country into a strong one. He added to his empire the lands of Edom, Moab and Ammon on the east bank of the Jordan.

Solomon

On David's death the kingdom passed to his son Solomon. David had many wives and concubines, and Solomon's mother was Bathsheba, a beautiful woman whom David married after contriving for her husband to be killed in battle. Bathsheba was an ambitious mother, and she persuaded David to

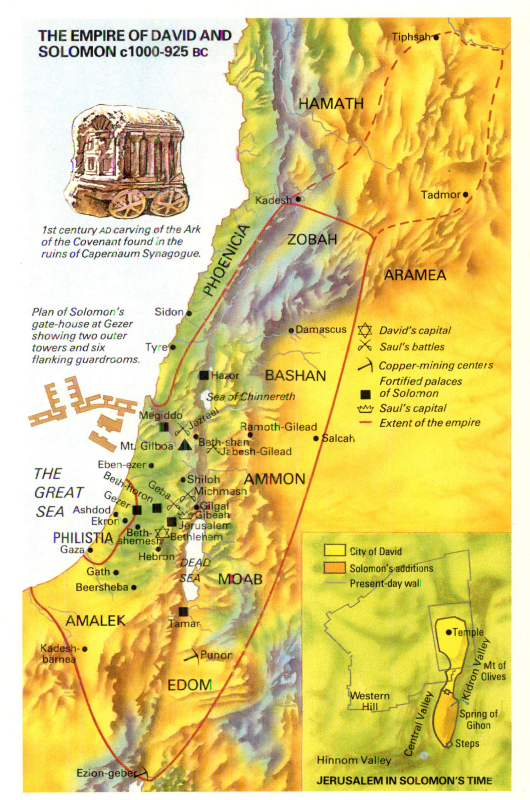

THE EMPIRE OF DAVID AND SOLOMON c1000-925 BC

1st century AD carving of the Ark of the Covenant found in the ruins of Capernaum Synagogue.

Plan of Solomon's gate-house at Gezer showing two outer towers and six flanking guardrooms.

✡ David's capital
✗ Saul's battles
⌐ Copper-mining centers
■ Fortified palaces of Solomon
♔ Saul's capital
— Extent of the empire

JERUSALEM IN SOLOMON'S TIME

☐ City of David
☐ Solomon's additions
— Present-day wall

Temple
Mt of Olives
Western Hill
Central Valley
Kidron Valley
Spring of Gihon
Steps
Hinnom Valley

nominate Solomon as his successor. Solomon was a skillful diplomat with a reputation for wisdom, but during his reign we read of luxury and forced labor. He did not add to David's kingdom, but he kept it together and made it more wealthy. Solomon spent much of this wealth in building. The most important of his buildings was the Temple in Jerusalem, which stood where the Mosque of Omar now stands. Solomon also had a trading arrangement with the Phoenician king of Tyre, Hiram, which brought more wealth to the Israelites. The Phoenician ships traded in the Mediterranean. With Solomon's help they also sailed to Africa and eastern Asia, using a port at Ezion-geber. The site of Ezion-geber has not yet been found, but it was probably near present-day Eilat on the Gulf of Aqaba.

The solid line marks the limits of David's kingdom, while the dotted line to the north shows territories which were under Solomon's influence.

Journey of the Ark of the Covenant

After the conquest of Canaan and before Solomon built the Temple which gave the Ark a place to "rest for ever", it was placed in a tabernacle at Shiloh and carried with the Israelites wherever they went. This is the route the Ark took:

Shiloh to **Eben-ezer,** where it was captured by the Philistines and taken to **Ashdod.** Plague and disaster struck the Philistines so they took the Ark to **Gath** and then **Ekron.** Disaster continued, so they carried it to **Beth-shemesh** in Judah and returned it to the Israelites. They took it to **Kirjath-jearim** where it stayed for 20 years before David brought it to **Jerusalem.**

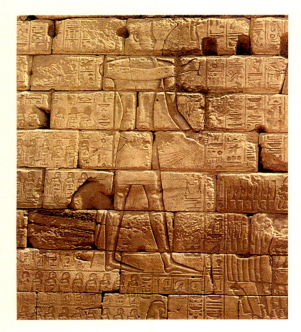

The victories of Pharaoh Sheshonk I are recorded in this relief, carved on the south wall of the Temple of Karnak in Egypt. The large figure is the god Amon, leading the 138 cities of Judah which Sheshonk captured. Each city is represented by a figure labeled with its name in hieroglyphics (picture writing).

Division and Defeat

I Kings 12-end
II Kings 1-17
II Chronicles 10-28

A great deal of the country's wealth went to Solomon's court, creating a class structure of rich and poor people. When Solomon died the ten northern tribes broke away and formed their own kingdom of Israel. Solomon's son Rehoboam was left to rule over the southern kingdom of Judah.

Judah and Israel quarreled and fought for nearly all of their 250-year history. But the real threat to both countries was from outside, from the countries surrounding Palestine.

The first attack came during the fifth year of the reign of Rehoboam. The armies of Pharaoh Sheshonk I of Egypt (called Shishak in the Bible) swept through the land, plundering as they went. They took away the golden treasures of the Temple in Jerusalem, which had to be replaced with the cheaper bronze. An inscription on the wall of the Temple of Karnak in Egypt also records the raid and lists the cities which were devastated. Many cities in Israel were among those raided.

The ten tribes which made up Israel quarreled among themselves as well as with Judah. Jeroboam, Israel's leader, wanted to discourage his people from regarding the Temple of Solomon in Jerusalem as the center of their religion. So he set up two

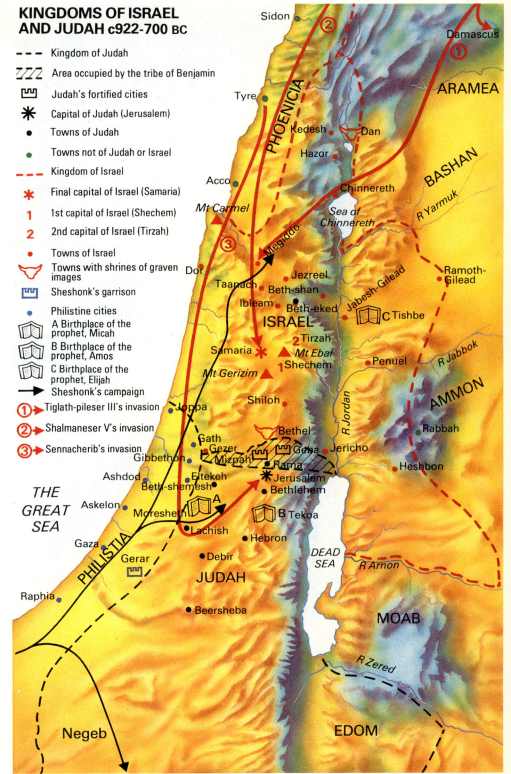

KINGDOMS OF ISRAEL AND JUDAH c922-700 BC

- – – – Kingdom of Judah
- ZZZ Area occupied by the tribe of Benjamin
- Judah's fortified cities
- ✳ Capital of Judah (Jerusalem)
- • Towns of Judah
- • Towns not of Judah or Israel
- – – – Kingdom of Israel
- ✳ Final capital of Israel (Samaria)
- 1 1st capital of Israel (Shechem)
- 2 2nd capital of Israel (Tirzah)
- • Towns of Israel
- Towns with shrines of graven images
- Sheshonk's garrison
- • Philistine cities
- A Birthplace of the prophet, Micah
- B Birthplace of the prophet, Amos
- C Birthplace of the prophet, Elijah
- → Sheshonk's campaign
- ①→ Tiglath-pileser III's invasion
- ②→ Shalmaneser V's invasion
- ③→ Sennacherib's invasion

new shrines, each containing the gilded image of a calf. One shrine was at Bethel, near the border with Judah. The other was at Dan in the extreme north of the country (the tribe of Dan had migrated there from their original lands in the southwest).

Omri, the great king of Israel, founded a new capital city at Samaria, 13 kilometers (8 miles) north of Shechem. He overran the land of Moab, east of the Jordan, and in a stone inscription found there, King Mesha of Moab records Omri's eventual defeat. This is the first real reference by name to a Hebrew king in the chronicles of other lands. Omri's son Ahab was a warrior, married to a Phoenician princess, Jezebel. Ahab and Jezebel introduced the worship of Baal to Israel. For this they were denounced by the religious leader Elijah, a

The kingdoms of Israel and Judah as they were divided up after the death of Solomon. The area between the two was occupied by the warlike tribe of Benjamin, which was fought over by the two kingdoms for many years. The map also shows the Egyptian and Assyrian campaigns to invade Palestine.

Take away from me the noise of your songs;
to the melody of your harps
I will not listen.
But let justice roll down like waters,
and righteousness like an
everflowing stream.
Amos 5: 23-24

reformer and prophet of great influence.

In 854 BC the Assyrian king Shalmaneser III attacked the coastal lands of the Mediterranean. Ahab joined a coalition with King Ben-hadad of Damascus (Syria) and his name is recorded in Shalmaneser's own account of the campaign. But Ahab later fell out with Ben-hadad and was killed in battle against him.

Ahab's son Joram was overthrown by one of his generals, Jehu, who massacred the Baal-worshipers in the name of Yahweh, an act of blood for which he was later condemned by the prophet Hosea. However, Jehu lost a great deal of his kingdom and had to pay homage to Shalmaneser III to keep the rest of it. This is recorded in a carving found in the Assyrian city of Nimrud.

The Prophets

Israel enjoyed one last spell of peace and prosperity, during the long reign of Jeroboam II (786-746 BC). During his reign we encounter the first of that remarkable series of inspired men we call the prophets. He was Amos, a shepherd from Tekoa, who in the name of Yahweh demanded justice for the poor. There had been earlier prophets, but we have only oral traditions about them. Amos was the first of a great succession who had their oracles written down. During the eighth century there were also Hosea the prophet of tender love, Isaiah, with his vision of the holiness of God and God's kingdom, and Micah.

Two years before Jeroboam II died Tiglath-pileser III, a brutal conqueror also known as Pul, became king of Assyria. He threatened Israel, Judah and other western lands and made them pay him money to leave them alone. But in 732 BC, at the request of Judah's king Ahaz, he invaded Israel, laid it waste, and deported many of its people. Hoshea, the last king of Israel, ruled over a small remnant of the land. He tried to rebel against the Assyrians but was taken prisoner. The mighty city of Samaria withstood a siege for two years. When it fell in 722 BC, the land of Israel ceased to exist. The Assyrian king, Sargon II, took away 29,290 captives and resettled the land with people from Arabia, Babylonia and Syria.

Ahaz of Judah had asked the Assyrians for help because he was being attacked. As a result of Ahaz's action Judah became a state belonging to Assyria, although it retained some independence.

This drawing, based on Assyrian carvings, shows how the Assyrians carried out a siege, such as the one which overcame Samaria in 722 BC. The besiegers advance, protected by shields against the hail of stones and arrows which the Jewish defenders rain down on them. On the left an armored battering ram, hammers slowly away at the huge walls.

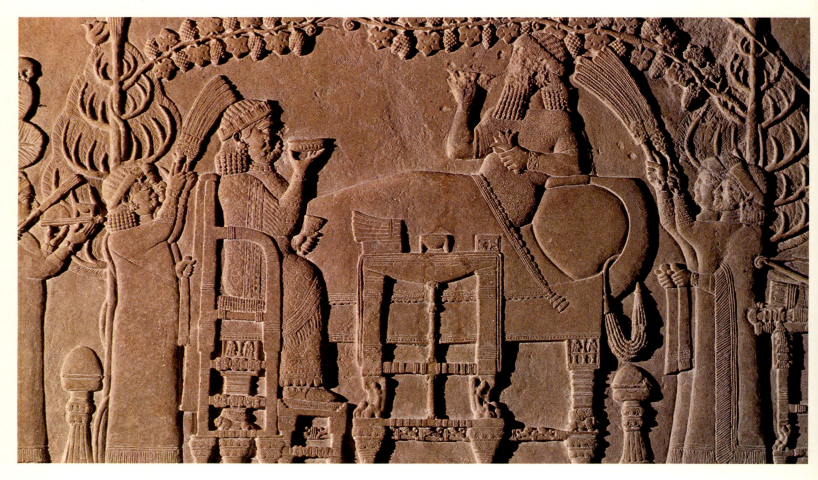

The Babylonian Captivity

II Kings 18-end
II Chronicles 29-end

An Assyrian relief showing King Asshurbanipal and his wife, Asshursharrat, having a feast under the vine. It was to celebrate his victory over the Elamites at the battle of Susa in 655 BC. With his right hand he raises a goblet of wine to his lips. Beside the couch is a table with food. By modern Western standards people in the Middle East tended to have a comparatively simple diet, with the emphasis on bread and fruit. Meat was used sparingly, mainly because in a hot climate it did not keep well. Onions and lentils were popular vegetables.

The years following the destruction of Israel were difficult ones for the state of Judah. King Hezekiah at first did nothing to upset the Assyrians. But when a new king, Sennacherib, came to the throne of Assyria in 705 BC, Hezekiah made an alliance with the Egyptians, Phoenicians and Philistines, and these western states rebelled against the power of Assyria.

At the time Sennacherib was occupied with a rebellion in the eastern part of his large empire. In 701 BC, with the eastern rebellion over, he swept down on the western alliance. He quickly defeated Judah's allies, captured 46 walled cities in Judah and shut up Hezekiah in Jerusalem "like a bird in a cage". This phrase occurs in an inscription which Sennacherib himself had made to describe his deeds. Besides Jerusalem, only the fortress city of Lachish held out. Assyrian wall-carvings, now in the British Museum, tell the story of that siege. The Assyrians used siege engines, armored battering-rams, to hammer at the walls, while archers kept up a storm of arrows. The Israelites showered the attackers with stones, arrows and blazing torches.

The frightened Hezekiah offered Sennacherib all the gold and silver he had left if he would leave Judah in peace. The Assyrian king demanded complete surrender and began to besiege Jerusalem. Then he suddenly broke off the siege and went back to Assyria. The people of Judah believed that they had been saved by God.

The Assyrian Empire Crumbles

Until about 632 BC the kings of Judah had no power of their own and did what their Assyrian masters told them. But the Assyrians began to lose their grip on their empire, under a succession of weak kings. King Josiah (640-609 BC) took advantage of this weakness to invade part of the old Israelite territory and to occupy part of the Philistine seacoast. He also threw off the Assyrian religion which had been imposed on the country and reintroduced traditional Jewish worship.

The end of Assyria's wealth and power came more quickly than anyone would have expected. When its last great king, Asshurbanipal, died in 627 BC the country was still strong, though less powerful than it had been. Trouble came from the southern land of Babylonia, which had been in Assyrian control for many years. Nabopolassar, who was governor of the Babylonian province of Chaldea, began it. In 626 BC he made himself king of Babylonia and began a revolt against the rulers of Assyria. He was supported by King Cyaxares of Media. Together the Babylonians and the Medes overran

Assyria. The Assyrian capital, Nineveh, was destroyed in 612 BC and was never rebuilt.

In 609 BC the last Assyrian army made a desperate attempt to recapture Haran, the city where the patriarch Abraham had spent several years. Pharaoh Necho of Egypt led an army northward to help them. Josiah tried to stop this support reaching the Assyrians, his hated enemies. With his army he gave battle to the Egyptians at Megiddo but was defeated and killed. Necho swept on through Syria, but was finally stopped at Carchemish, whose ruins now lie close to the Turkish border. There a Babylonian army led by Nabopolassar's son Nebuchadnezzar defeated him in 605 BC. Soon afterwards Nebuchadnezzar succeeded his father as king.

Nebuchadnezzar

Nebuchadnezzar spent some time making Babylon, the capital of his new and mighty empire, into the most beautiful city of the world. He laid out the city with broad, well-paved roads, lined with large buildings. Because his wife, the Princess Amytis of Media, came from a mountainous land and found the flat Babylonian plain dull, the king built the legendary "Hanging Gardens of Babylon", with trees and plants growing on some form of artificial hill. But he did not forget the people in his state of Judah.

In 601 King Jehoiakim of Judah began a rebellion. Three years later Nebuchadnezzar led an expedition to Judah. Jehoiakim died before the Babylonian armies arrived, and left his 18-year-old son Jehoiachin in charge. After only three months on the throne he was forced to surrender to the Babylonians. Nebuchadnezzar took him and 10,000 of his subjects back to Babylon as prisoners. Nebuchadnezzar installed Jehoiachin's uncle, Zedekiah, as king.

Nine years later Zedekiah rebelled against the Babylonians, with the support of the Egyptians. This time Nebuchadnezzar made no mistake. He captured Jerusalem and destroyed it. His troops set fire to the Temple of Solomon, the royal palace and all the houses, and pulled down the defensive walls of the city. Zedekiah was blinded and taken prisoner to Babylon, where he died. Nebuchadnezzar took thousands more Judeans off to Babylon. He left Judah under the rule of a governor, Gedaliah. Judean guerrillas killed the governor, and a third deportation of the population took place. A few escaped and fled to Egypt. Just 650 years after Joshua had led the Israelites to the Promised Land, the bulk of their descendants were gone from there.

The period up to the Exile and immediately after was the period of the great prophet Jeremiah, who for forty years warned the leaders against playing politics with the Great Powers instead of turning to God and his ways.

Kings of Judah under the rule of the Kings of Assyria and Babylon

Assyria: Sennacherib (705-681)
Hezekiah 715-687/6
Manasseh 687/6-642
Assyria: Esarhaddon (681-669)
Asshurbanipal (669-627)
Amon 642-640
Josiah 640-609
Babylon: Nabopolassar (626-605)
Jehoahaz 609
Jehoiakim 609-598
Babylon: Nebuchadnezzar (605-562)
Jehoiachin 598-597
Zedekiah 597-587

Below: A reconstruction of the magnificent Ishtar gate at Babylon. The gate was dedicated to the goddess Ishtar. It was one of the great ceremonial entrances to the city in Nebuchadnezzar's time, and led to a broad road used for processions. The gateway is covered with colored glazed bricks, with dragons and bulls moulded in relief. The original gate is now in a museum of oriental art in Berlin.

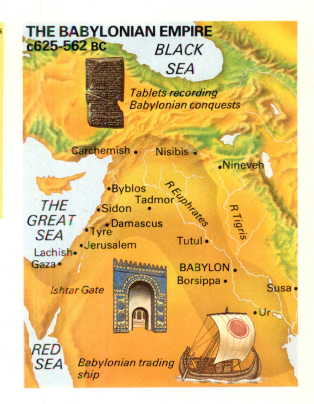

THE BABYLONIAN EMPIRE c625-562 BC

Tablets recording Babylonian conquests

Babylonian trading ship

Above: This map shows the gradual spread of Babylonian power until it swept through the Fertile Crescent to include Palestine and the whole of the eastern Mediterranean coast.

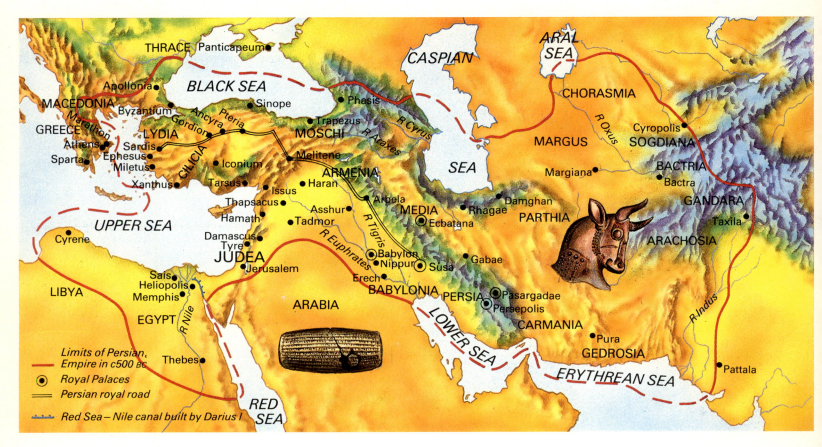

The Return

Ezra
Nehemiah
Esther

The Israelites who had gone from and returned to Jerusalem and Judea after their exile were now known as Jews. Their captivity in Babylon had lasted less than 50 years, barely two generations.

For many of the Jews it was a very comfortable exile. They were living in or near one of the biggest and most sophisticated cities of the Middle East. They were able to build houses and cultivate the land, while the members of the royal family were entertained at court. However, they could not forget their homeland, as the opening of the 137th Psalm makes clear:

By the rivers of Babylon we sat down and wept
*   when we remembered Zion.*
There on the willow-trees
*   we hung up our harps,*
for there those who carried us off
*   demanded music and singing*
and our captors called on us to be merry:
*   'Sing us one of the songs of Zion.'*
How could we sing the Lord's song
*   in a foreign land?*

The exiles spent a great deal of time thinking about not only their homeland but also their religion. This period saw the great prophecies of Ezekiel and (as most scholars think) of an unknown prophet whose words are preserved in *Isaiah 40-59*. The Babylonian ruler Nabonidus, who came to the throne in 556 BC, has been called "the first archaeologist", because he had the ruins of ancient buildings dug up. Nabonidus spent more time studying than ruling and left the

government of the country largely to his son, Belshazzar.

Cyrus the Great

While the Babylonian ruler was thinking of the past, the present was catching up with him. Cyrus, the king of Anshan, in Persia was rising rapidly to power. He succeeded to the throne of Anshan in 558 BC, and brought Media and Persia under control by 550 BC, and then turned his attention to Babylonia. In 539 BC his troops marched into Babylon, which surrendered without a struggle. Babylonia became a Persian province. Just 22 years after Nebuchadnezzar died, leaving Babylonia as the most powerful country in the Middle East, his empire had ceased to exist.

The Persian Empire at its greatest extent in about 500 BC, during the reign of Darius I. It extended from Greece and Egypt in the west to what is now the frontier between Afghanistan and Pakistan. It was crossed by roads, along which messengers sped with dispatches to the outposts of the empire. The principal road was the so-called Royal Road, from Susa in the southeast to the Aegean Sea. Darius also had a canal cut from the Red Sea to the River Nile. The inset pictures show a huge bull's head which adorned the top of a pillar in the royal palace at Susa, Darius's winter residence. On the clay cylinder Cyrus the Great recorded how he liberated his captives, including the Jews.

Tomb of Cyrus the Great at Pasargadae, Iran from c 530 BC.

CYRUS THE GREAT

Cyrus II, called the Great, ruled over the Persian empire for 29 years until he died in 530 BC. His father was Cambyses I, king of Anshan, whom he succeeded in 559 BC. By 540 BC he had conquered the whole of western Asia and created the Persian empire. Cyrus was a skillful politician as well as an intrepid soldier. He knew how to keep his subject peoples happy, which he did partly by a policy of religious toleration. Many historians, including Herodotus the Greek, record the life and achievements of this great king. He was killed on an expedition to the East and was buried in a small simple stone tomb near his palace at Pasargadae, in southern Iran. The tomb, now empty, still stands.

The arrival of Cyrus the Great – as he was later known – was fortunate for the Jews. Cyrus was a brilliantly farsighted monarch who instead of repressing and bullying his empire states chose to liberate them. He changed laws and edicts made by his generals at the moment of conquest to make his subjects' lives more tolerable. The most important quality that he possessed as far as the Jews were concerned was his belief that local religious cults should be allowed to flourish. This was a reversal of the Assyrian and Babylonian attitude.

Imagine the reception he received on entering Babylon. He was fêted as a liberator not feared as a conqueror. So acceptable was he to the Babylonian people that he took the place of Marduk – the chief God of Babylon – in the famous New Year Procession through the Ishtar Gate thus giving him a divine right to rule. On his arrival he found a number of captive peoples living in Babylon. He promptly sent them home. He describes this act on a clay cylinder found in the ruins of Babylon, which also records how he captured the city. Among the peoples allowed to return to their homelands, if they wanted to, were the Jews. What is more, he ordered all the sacred vessels looted from the Temple at Jerusalem to be returned.

But when Sheshbazzar, who was most probably a son of King Jehoaichin, set off in 538 BC only a few exiles joined him, most preferring to stay in Babylonia where they had houses and land which they were not prepared to exchange for an insecure future in Palestine. But they did support the returning party with money and supplies.

Starting Again

Bitter though exile had been, the Jews' homecoming was still harder. Jerusalem lay in ruins. Other tribes had moved into large areas of Judea. To the north the people of the former kingdom of Israel, which contained a large number of foreign settlers, were partly friendly and partly hostile. There were also certain Jews who had escaped deportation and remained in Judea. In these circumstances the returning exiles found it very difficult to settle down. They quickly set up a new altar in the ruins of Solomon's Temple, and began holding religious services there. But they did not get very far with rebuilding the temple itself. It was in fact 23 years before the work was finished. The city walls lay in ruins for another 70 years. This work was particularly hindered by the people of the former Israel, who had been left behind, now known as Samaritans after the name of their capital, Samaria. Meanwhile thousands of Jews toiled across the desert from Babylon, back to Judea in a series of camel caravans taking with them about 7000 slaves. The Jews must have done well in Babylon to possess so many slaves.

In 444 BC a Jewish official at the Persian court, Nehemiah, was sent to Jerusalem as governor. This was at his own request, because he was disturbed by the reports of Jerusalem's disorganized state. Three days after his arrival he made a moonlight inspection of the walls. Then he called the people together and persuaded them to get busy on repairs. The Samaritans harassed the workers, so Nehemiah posted an armed guard. The work was finished in just over seven weeks. Nehemiah posted a permanent resident garrison in the city.

Nehemiah was a tremendous organizer. It was Nehemiah who ensured that the Jewish Law known as the *Torah*, was strictly enforced. (It applied to Jews living in Exile as well as those in Judea.) He was aided by Ezra, a priest who had returned from exile in Babylon with another party of Jews.

The Bible story of the Jews ends with the return to Judea and the activities of Ezra and Nehemiah. Nehemiah paid a second visit to Jerusalem in 432 BC. After that we know hardly anything about what happened during the next hundred years. Judea remained a Persian province, governed by a succession of high priests. Samaria had its own governors and was administered as a separate province. In 362 BC a number of Phoenician cities rebelled against Persian rule, and the Persian expedition to quell the revolt must have affected Judea. Remains of buildings of the period have been found by the archaeologists. The primitive foundations, badly made bricks and lack of ornament and decoration show that the people had a relatively poor life. The only surviving evidence of the period is revealed by coins, issued by the various high priests, bearing the name of the province in Hebrew script.

Some of the might of the kings of Persia is shown in this sculptured relief of the royal guard at Persepolis. The ruins of this splendid city lie in southwestern Iran. It was built by Cyrus the Great's son-in-law, Darius I. The Persian kings were very conscious of their power: an inscription found on a clay cylinder reads: "I am Cyrus, king of all, the great king, the mighty king . . . king of the four corners of the Earth".

Between the Testaments

Much of the story of the Bible lands between the end of the Old Testament narrative and the beginning of the New Testament story comes from non-Jewish sources. However, some of it is told in two books of the Apocrypha. The Apocrypha, which means "hidden" or "spurious" in Greek, is a group of religious writings which are not included in the Hebrew Bible used by the Jews. Two of these books are historical accounts, the First and Second Books of the Maccabees.

Alexander the Great

When Cyrus the Great's descendant, Darius III, came to the throne of Persia in 335 BC, the Persian empire seemed as strong and as large as ever. But a new threat came from the northwest in the person of Alexander the Great, the young king of Macedonia in Greece. In October 333 BC he met Darius III in a pitched battle at Issus, (now in Southern Turkey), and beat him. He then marched down the eastern coast of the Mediterranean Sea, through Phoenicia, to Egypt. Alexander took possession of this Persian province and was hailed by the Egyptians as their new king. He finished the conquest of Persia the following year. Alexander treated the Jews well, and they submitted to their new master.

In 323 BC Alexander died, and his empire crumbled as quickly as he had set it up. His principal generals quarreled among themselves, and each took over part of the empire. One of them, Ptolemy, took control of Egypt and became ruler.

The old Babylonian empire came under the control of yet another Macedonian soldier, Seleucus.

One of the main results of the Greek conquests was the spread of Greek ways of life and ideas and the use of the Greek language. Greek, indeed, became a sort of international language, much as English did in the days of the British Empire. Many Jews in Alexandria spoke Greek rather than Hebrew, and in the 200s BC the whole of the Old Testament was translated into Greek for them to use. This translation is known as the Septuagint (from the Latin word for seventy) because according to legend 72 translators worked on it.

In 175 BC Antiochus IV became ruler of the Seleucid empire. He was an eccentric man, who wanted to turn Judea (as Judah was then called) into a completely Greek state. He was helped in this work by two

"Alexander of Macedon, the son of Philip, marched from the land of Kittim, defeated Darius, king of Persia and Media, and seized his throne..." These, the opening words of the First Book of the Maccabees in the Apocrypha, might have been written to describe this mosaic picture found in the ruins of the Roman city of Pompeii. This mosaic, made about 100 BC, is thought to be a copy of a much older Greek work. The fiery Alexander is shown on the left, while on the right the fleeing Darius III looks anxiously back from his chariot. The battle shown is that fought at Issus in 333 BC.

The Kingdom of the Maccabees under the rule of John Hyrcanus and his immediate successors (134-63 BC). It covered almost the same area as in the great days of Solomon. The inset pictures show a bronze lamp found in Syria, decorated with Jewish religious symbols; and a Jewish coin issued during the rule of Simon Maccabeus (142-134 BC).

unscrupulous high priests, Jason and his successor Menelaus. The Temple was converted to the worship of the chief Greek god, Zeus. The flesh of pigs – an abomination to every right-thinking Jew – was offered up on the altar as a sacrifice. The Jews were forbidden to follow their own ways of worship on pain of death.

The Maccabees

The Jews had put up with a great deal from their successive conquerors. But when the soldiers of Antiochus tried to set up a pagan altar in his home town of Modin, an old priest named Mattathias killed the first Jew who went to the altar to sacrifice and the officer in command. Mattathias then led the resulting revolt and with his five sons, John, Simon, Judah (Judas in Greek), Eleazar and Jonathan, he escaped to the hills.

After Mattathias died Judah, nicknamed the Maccabee (the Hammer), took over the leadership of the guerrillas. The five brothers, known as Hasmoneans because they came of the family of Hasmon, set out to win complete independence for Judea. Eleazar and Judah were both killed in battle, and Jonathan took over the command. John died soon after in an ambush. Jonathan became high priest and head of state. His career was ended by a Greek general named Tryphon, who invited him to a conference and then killed him by treachery. So Simon, the last of the brothers, became high priest and ruler of Judea.

After seven years in office, Simon was killed by his son-in-law, an ambitious man named Ptolemeus, who wanted to seize power. Ptolemeus's plans were foiled by Simon's son, John Hyrcanus, who was commander-in-chief of the Judean army. John took over the government of the land, and when the empire of the Seleucids collapsed in 129 BC, he was able to make Judea free and independent once again. John and his immediate successors extended the frontiers of Judea, until it was about the same size as it had been in the great days of David and Solomon.

By this time the Jewish faith consisted of three main sects or groups. The Sadducees believed that only the written scriptures contained the true Law of God. They were politically powerful and opposed religious narrowness. The Pharisees believed that a great deal of oral tradition – that is, the spoken word – was also the Law of God. They were pious and strict in their religious way of life. They were also active in improving the lot of their followers. The third group, the Essenes, were a very strict sect who lived in isolated communities, leading a life of self-denial and hard work. One of their main colonies was in the mountains on the shores of the Dead Sea. There in 1947 a collection of their books and documents, known as the Dead Sea Scrolls, was found.

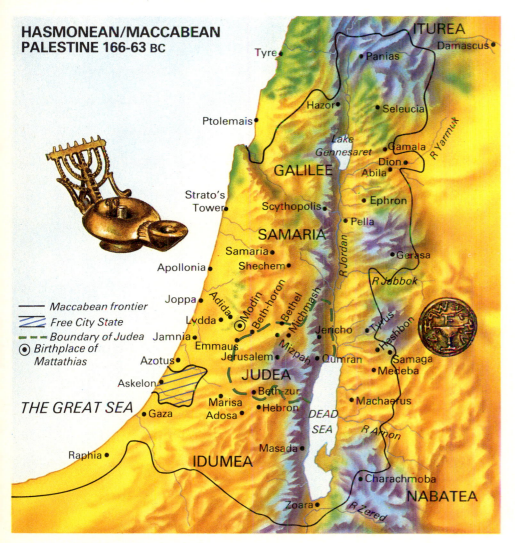

HASMONEAN/MACCABEAN PALESTINE 166-63 BC

ITUREA
Damascus
Tyre
Panias
Hazor
Seleucia
Ptolemais
R Yarmuk
Lake Gennesaret
Gamala
GALILEE
Dion
Abila
Strato's Tower
Ephron
Scythopolis
Pella
SAMARIA
R Jordan
Samaria
Gerasa
Apollonia
Shechem
R Jabbok
Joppa
Adida
Modin
Beth-horon
Bethel
Michmash
Lydda
Jericho
Jamnia
Emmaus
Mizpah
Jerusalem
Qumran
Samaga
Azotus
Medeba
Heshbon
R Titus
JUDEA
Beth-zur
Askelon
Marisa
Hebron
Machaerus
Adosa
DEAD SEA
THE GREAT SEA
Gaza
R Arnon
Masada
Raphia
IDUMEA
Charachmoba
NABATEA
Zoara
R Zered

— Maccabean frontier
⫽ Free City State
- - - Boundary of Judea
◉ Birthplace of Mattathias

The Roman Conquest

Family quarrels marred the story of John Hyrcanus's descendants. There were also sharp religious differences. John's sons, Aristobulus and Alexander Janneus both supported the Sadducees, who were concerned with worldly matters more than spiritual ones. Since the king was also high priest, his non-religious attitude angered the Pharisees. Alexander Janneus was an unscrupulous, bloodthirsty and savage king. His contempt for the Pharisees led to a civil war, which he won.

Hyrcanus II became priest-king in 67 BC, but was immediately deposed by his warlike younger brother Aristobulus II. Hyrcanus fled to Syria and asked its king, Aretas, for help.

Pompey the Great

Meanwhile the Roman general Gnaeus Pompeius Magnus – Pompey the Great – arrived in Judea. The rival brothers both appealed to Pompey for support. The Pharisees also appealed to him, asking the Romans to abolish the monarchy and let Judea be governed by the priests. In 63 BC Pompey marched into Jerusalem with his well-disciplined legions. Pompey abolished the monarchy, but left Hyrcanus to rule as high priest. However, only some of the Jews lived in Judea. Over the years many had emigrated. The Jews were able merchants, and they settled in foreign lands in order to carry on trading. They were found in small colonies in all the Mediterranean lands. After Pompey's arrival in Jerusalem, a small colony of Jews was established in Rome. They took with them their religious faith, but they all looked to Jerusalem as their religious center.

The End of the Maccabees

The high priest Hyrcanus was a man of a rather simple nature. He was strongly influenced by his friend Antipater, a wealthy man of Arab descent who had been converted to Judaism. Antipater was governor of Idumea, and in time became the effective ruler of all Judea. He was a very clever politician and always contrived to keep on good terms with the current government. As a result he was eventually rewarded with Roman citizenship, which gave its owner relief from certain taxes and other privileges. It also passed on to one's children. Antipater was poisoned by a rival in 43 BC, and his son, Herod, took over his duties. He soon persuaded Hyrcanus to relinquish his remaining power and with his brother, Phezahel, ruled Judea for the Romans.

For a time Hyrcanus's nephew, Antigonus,

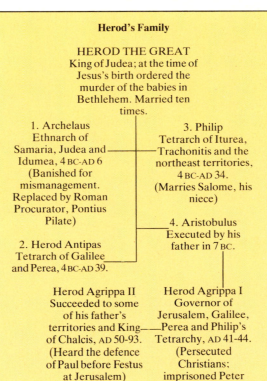

Herod's Family

HEROD THE GREAT
King of Judea; at the time of Jesus's birth ordered the murder of the babies in Bethlehem. Married ten times.

1. **Archelaus** Ethnarch of Samaria, Judea and Idumea, 4 BC-AD 6 (Banished for mismanagement. Replaced by Roman Procurator, Pontius Pilate)

2. **Herod Antipas** Tetrarch of Galilee and Perea, 4 BC-AD 39.

3. **Philip** Tetrarch of Iturea, Trachonitis and the northeast territories, 4 BC-AD 34. (Marries Salome, his niece)

4. **Aristobulus** Executed by his father in 7 BC.

Herod Agrippa II Succeeded to some of his father's territories and King of Chalcis, AD 50-93. (Heard the defence of Paul before Festus at Jerusalem)

Herod Agrippa I Governor of Jerusalem, Galilee, Perea and Philip's Tetrarchy, AD 41-44. (Persecuted Christians; imprisoned Peter and executed James)

Above: The Herodium, near Bethlehem, is one of the many fortresses built by Herod the Great, probably with the idea that they would make places of refuge in the event of civil war. The courtyard is reached by a long ramp and a staircase. Herod seems to have intended this for his tomb.

Far right: The "Wailing Wall" in Jerusalem is one of the few remaining parts of Herod's Temple. It formed the western supporting wall of the courtyard. It gets its modern name from the fact that, for many years, Jews have gone here to pray and to mourn the destruction of the Temple.

Below: The Roman Empire at its greatest extent, under the Emperor Trajan (AD 98-117). The inset pictures show a Roman soldier; the Pont du Gard, a Roman aqueduct which still stands near Nimes, in France; Trajan's column, in Rome, which recorded his triumphs in Palestine; a Roman ship; and a coin bearing the emperor's head.

THE ROMAN EMPIRE cAD 117

London
Paris
Augsburg
BLACK SEA
R Danube
Budapest
Tamar
Milan
Bordeaux
Sardis
Antioch
Massilia
ROME
Athens
Pompeii
Damascus
Caesaraugusta
Carthage
Alexandria
Lisbon
Cordoba
Cyrene
R Nile
Timgad
Leptis Magna

seized power. So Herod went to Rome, where he won the support of Julius Caesar's immediate successors, Marcus Antonius and Octavius Caesar. They made him King of Judea in 37 BC. Soon after this he married Hyrcanus's granddaughter, Mariamne.

The Nativity

According to the New Testament of the Bible, Jesus Christ was born in Bethlehem in the last years of Herod's reign, probably in either 6 or 5 BC. (The reason why Jesus was born "before Christ" is that when the years from his birth were calculated in the AD 500s the monk Dionysius Exiguus, who carried out the work, made a mistake in his sums.) Mary and Joseph, the carpenter, lived in Nazareth. According to the Bible, Emperor Augustus needed a census taken so ". . . that all the world should be taxed". For this purpose all citizens had to return to their ancestral homes. Joseph's family line was of the House of David of Bethlehem. So Joseph and Mary, who was in the last stages of pregnancy, set off on the 128 kilometer (80 mile) journey to Bethlehem.

Exhausted after their journey, Mary gave birth to Joshua, Jesus being the Greek form of the name, meaning "God saves", in a stable, the only accommodation available in the crowded and bustling Bethlehem.

The Three Wise Men

Soon after Jesus was born, the three Magi – thought to be members of a caste of Persian astrologers or magicians known for their wisdom, hence the three Wise Men – saw a bright star which they followed west to Jerusalem. There have been various explanations for the divine star – a bright meteor, a comet, a new star – but the unusual meeting of Saturn, Jupiter and Mars in late February, 6 BC seems to fit historically; it would also generate enough light to be startling.

When they arrived in Jerusalem, they asked "Where is he that is born King of the Jews?". Herod heard of this. He asked the foreigners to report Jesus's whereabouts supposedly so that he could worship Jesus, too. The Wise Men left and soon they saw the bright star over Bethlehem. They followed the star the 8 kilometers (5 miles) to Bethlehem where they saw Jesus and rejoiced. That night God warned them in a dream not to tell Herod where Jesus was, so instead the Wise Men left for Persia by a different road.

Two years later Herod had still heard no news of Jesus's whereabouts, so he ordered all the children in Bethlehem under two years old to be killed. Joseph, meanwhile had been told by God in a dream to escape with Mary and Jesus to Egypt. So in the middle of the night Joseph took them on a donkey, the 400 kilometers (250 miles) into Egypt. They remained there until Herod died a short while later.

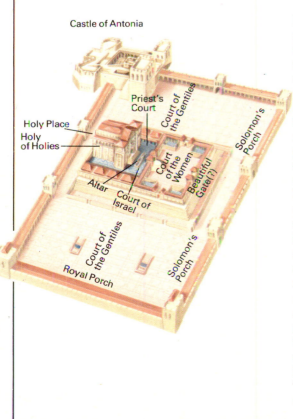

Castle of Antonia

Priest's Court

Holy Place
Holy of Holies

Court of the Gentiles

Solomon's Porch

Altar

Court of Israel

Court of the Women

Beautiful Gate (?)

Court of the Gentiles

Royal Porch

Solomon's Porch

HEROD'S TEMPLE

Herod was a gentile and needed to placate his Jewish subjects, so he built them this magnificent Temple at Jerusalem. Gentiles were forbidden to enter the inner courts on pain of death. The old Temple, built by the Jews on their return from Babylon, had been raided many times and was probably in poor condition. The new Temple was a much more magnificent structure than the old one, though it was probably about the same size. However, the new buildings were higher than the old ones. Herod had huge courtyards built around the Temple in order to accommodate all the pilgrims who came to worship there. Although most of the work was completed in about 18 months, construction of the outer courtyards continued until the AD 60s. In AD 70 the Temple was destroyed. Only a few parts of it remain, among them the so-called "Wailing Wall" which formed part of the outer terracing.

Where Jesus Preached

Matthew 1-25
Mark 1-10
Luke 1-21
John 1-10

Herod was probably the cleverest and most capable ruler the Jews ever had. At the same time he was cold and utterly ruthless. He had many potential rivals put to death. Among them were his brother-in-law, Aristobulus, whom he had made high priest; the aged Hyrcanus; 45 aristocratic friends of Antigonus; and later his wife Mariamne, her mother and their children. The king was hated, not only for his cruelty but also for his love for all things Greek.

Yet with all his faults Herod kept his kingdom at peace and made it prosperous. He kept the support and friendship of Emperor Augustus, and he supported the cause of Jews abroad.

After Herod's death in 4 BC Augustus divided the lands he ruled among three of his sons (see p.34). The century which followed was a fateful one for the Jews, because it saw the end of their country. It also saw the establishment of a new religion, Christianity, which has since spread all over the world. The events which began this new religion took place over a period of about 30 years, and their central point was a brief period of less than three years when Jesus preached his message.

Life in Palestine

The land into which Jesus was born was relatively peaceful. The towns were mostly Greek in character and contained many Greek-style buildings. His country even had a Greek name: Palaistine, from Philis-tine. People slept on low beds or cots. Their clothing was similar to that worn in Greece at the time – generally a *chiton* or tunic, with a mantle as a kind of cloak or over-garment, sandals for the feet and a hat or cap. Each community had its own synagogue, or local place of worship; large cities had several. In Jerusalem and the larger towns many of the upper classes were familiar with the Greek language. It was even used in the synagogues there. In the smaller towns the people spoke Aramaic, a language related to Hebrew, and widely used over a large part of the Middle East at that time. Jesus spoke Aramaic and a few of his words and phrases in that language were quoted in the original Greek of the New Testament. He said to Jairus's daughter, whom he had raised from the dead, "Talitha cumi" which means "Get up my child" (*Mark 5:41*).

Because the main events of the New Testament took place over a very short space of time and most of the main characters in the story were little-known people, there are very few archaeological remains to amplify the account. The destruction of the Jewish land and the dispersal of its inhabitants in AD 70 annihilated almost all traces of the people; even the synagogues of the day have not survived.

The Gospels

Our main sources for the life of Jesus are the four Biblical Gospels. They were all written within 60 years of Jesus's death and are based on a strong oral tradition. The Gospel of John appears to be an account derived from the Apostle John, probably the last survivor of those who had known Jesus well. In addition there are references to Christ and Christianity in the works of the Latin writers Tacitus and Suetonius, and of the Jewish historian Flavius Josephus, writing in Rome in AD 93. In general, there is no reason to doubt the main outlines of

A fisherman with his net, early in the morning on the Sea of Galilee. He is following a tradition which takes us back to the scene described in Matthew 4: 18-20. "Jesus was walking by the Sea of Galilee when he saw two brothers, Simon called Peter and his brother Andrew, casting a net into the lake, for they were fishermen".

the ministry of Jesus as presented in the gospels. These contrast with a number of legendary accounts of Jesus's life and sayings written somewhat later.

Jesus's Message

Apart from a visit to the Temple in Jerusalem when he was 12 years old, there is no other mention of Jesus until he was about 30 years old, when he began preaching. He gathered around him many disciples or followers. From them he chose 12 – the Twelve Apostles – to help him with his work.

The Romans had not yet introduced the broad, well-surfaced roads for which the empire was famous, and in Palestine the roadways along which Jesus walked or rode were still simple stony tracks, linking towns and villages. His days were taken up walking these roads, preaching, healing and praying. He was proclaiming "good news". "The Kingdom of God was at hand." But all the time Jesus was criticizing the religious leaders of the day. Inevitably he became a marked man. What particularly enraged the Pharisees and Sadducees were Jesus's miracles, because they were manifestations of Jesus's power over nature and therefore, in their eyes, blasphemy. But as Jesus explained behind his miracles or 'works' was a desire to be helpful to mankind.

In the desert one evening, Jesus had been preaching and his Apostles suggested that he send the multitude away to get a meal. But Jesus said "They need not go, they can eat what we have". "We have only five loaves and two fishes," was the Apostles' reply. "Bring them here," Jesus said, and looking up to Heaven he broke the loaves and blessed the fish and there was enough to feed everyone there.

That night his Apostles set off in a boat across the Sea of Galilee while Jesus prayed. At midnight Jesus went to them walking on the sea. They were frightened but Jesus urged Peter, one of his Apostles to come to him across the water. Peter set off confidently but became frightened and began to sink. Jesus saved him and admonished the disciples for having such little faith. They were ashamed, but replied "Of a truth, thou art the Messiah".

The Messiah

Ancient Jewish prophets had forecast the coming of a *Messiah* (an anointed one), a king who would bring peace to the Earth and salvation to the Jews. Jesus's followers firmly believed that he was that Messiah (in Greek, *Christos*). Other Jews did not accept him as the Messiah, and until his trial Jesus did not use the name in reference to himself. He preferred to call himself "the Son of Man" a phrase which occurs in the writings of many of the Old Testament prophets. At his trial he proclaimed he was the Messiah which had been prophesied in the book of Isaiah.

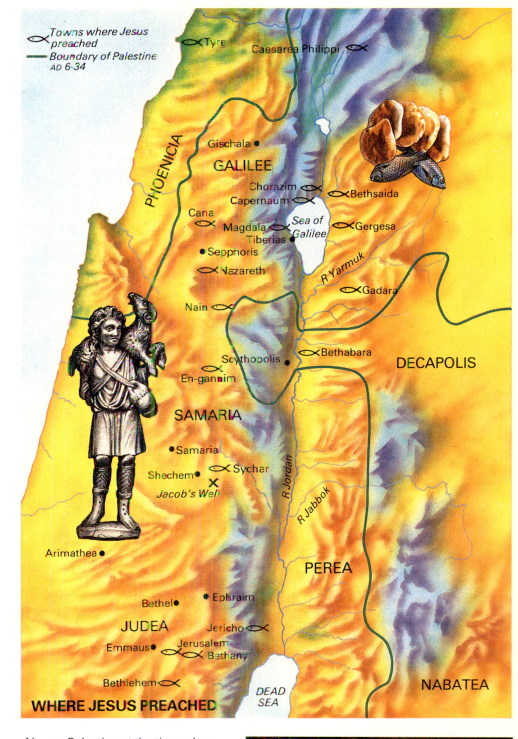

WHERE JESUS PREACHED

Towns where Jesus preached
Boundary of Palestine AD 6-34

Above: Palestine at the time when Jesus began his short-lived ministry. It shows the towns where he preached. Inset are the five loaves and two fishes of the Miracle at Bethsaida (recorded in Luke 9 and Mark 6), and an early Christian statue picturing Jesus as the Good Shepherd with a lamb.

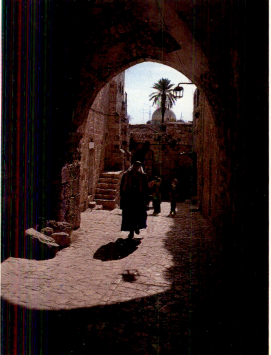

Right: An archway in the Old City of Jerusalem frames the Dome of the Rock in the background. Though the city has been rebuilt many times since the days of Jesus, it was through narrow streets like this that he would have approached the Temple, which stood where the Dome of the Rock now stands.

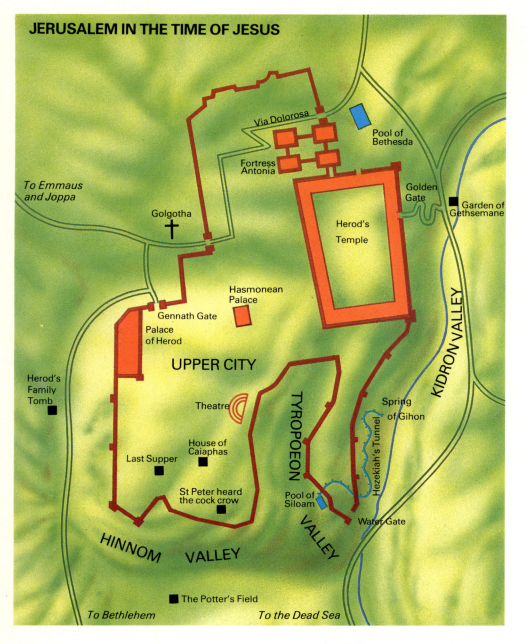

JERUSALEM IN THE TIME OF JESUS

Via Dolorosa

Pool of Bethesda

Fortress Antonia

Golden Gate

To Emmaus and Joppa

Garden of Gethsemane

Golgotha

Herod's Temple

KIDRON VALLEY

Hasmonean Palace

Gennath Gate

Palace of Herod

UPPER CITY

Herod's Family Tomb

Theatre

Spring of Gihon

TYROPOEON VALLEY

Hezekiah's Tunnel

House of Caiaphas

Last Supper

St Peter heard the cock crow

Pool of Siloam

Water Gate

HINNOM VALLEY

The Potter's Field

To Bethlehem

To the Dead Sea

Jerusalem at the time of Jesus's death was much larger than it had been in David's day, but it was still considerably smaller than the modern city. The Jerusalem Jesus knew was destroyed in AD 70 by the Romans – an event Jesus foretold (Mark 13). The Potter's Field, used for burying strangers, was the patch of land bought by the chief priests with the 30 pieces of silver that Judas cast at their feet in remorse.

Trial, Death and Resurrection

Matthew 26-end
Mark 11-end
Luke 22-end
John 11-end

There had been many instances of revolts led by religious extremists, later known as Zealots. The Zealots were a band of Jewish patriots dedicated to the liberation of Judea from Roman rule, and the Jewish and Roman authorities were nervous of these extremists.

Jesus knew that his person and his teaching were an offence to the Jewish establishment, he knew too that his revolutionary nature would lead to his execution by the Romans and foretold this. But he did not shrink from this moment of confrontation.

On the Saturday the week before the crucifixion Jesus had been preaching in

Jericho. He healed a blind man and then set off with his followers on the 32-kilometer (20-mile) journey for Bethany and Jerusalem. Their intention was to celebrate Passover which was due to begin the following Friday evening, coinciding with the start of the Sabbath, which lasts from dusk on Friday to dusk on Saturday. The journey though fairly short is very tiring. Jerusalem is 1000 meters (3300 feet) above Jericho. At Bethany, about 5 kilometers (3 miles) from Jerusalem they rested at Lazarus's house, the man whom Jesus had brought back to life a short time before. There they ate supper. The next day, Sunday, they set off. On the Mount of Olives, just east of Jerusalem, Jesus said to two of his disciples "Go into the next village and at its entrance you will find an ass tied. Untie it and bring it here. If any man asks you what you are doing, say, 'The Lord needs it'." They did this.

The event had been foretold in the book of *Zechariah (9:9)*: "Rejoice greatly, O daughter of Zion: shout, O daughter of Jerusalem: behold thy king cometh unto thee and riding upon an ass: and his dominion shall be from sea even to sea and from the river even to the ends of the Earth".

This is one of the many references to the coming of the Son of God and Messiah. In Jewish writings a fundamental belief was that a Messiah would come – a belief, therefore, shared by Jesus's followers. This is one of many reasons why Jesus's words were so powerful – the Word of the Lord, the Son of God. The Messiah had come.

The following day Jesus went to the Temple, still the most holy place in Jewish religious belief. It was full of traders selling doves and sheep for people to offer as their sacrifices. There were also money-changers who would, for a fee, change foreign currency into Jewish money. Foreign coins had the heads of kings or emperors on them and were considered graven images and unacceptable as payment to the Temple treasury. Jesus drove the traders out, saying "Scripture says, 'My house shall be called a house of prayer'; but you are making it a robbers' cave". This action further angered the priests.

The Betrayal

On Thursday, the eve of the Passover, Jesus and his followers ate the ritual Passover meal together. As the meal ended Judas Iscariot, one of the twelve Apostles, slipped away to see the high priest, Caiaphas. He offered to betray Jesus to the Jewish authorities and to point him out to the soldiers sent to arrest him. For this act Judas was paid 30 pieces of silver.

Jesus was arrested the same night. He was taken in front of the Sanhedrin, the Jewish supreme council, made up of 71 priests, elders and lawyers. The Sanhedrin

The Dome of the Rock in Jerusalem encloses the "Sacred Rock" from which, according to legend, Muhammad, the founder of Islam, ascended to Heaven in AD 632. This Muslim mosque is the latest in a succession of holy buildings on the site – the altar of David, Solomon's Temple, the later Temple built when the Jews returned from Babylon, Herod's Temple and a Temple to Jupiter built by the Roman emperor Hadrian. The Wailing Wall, part of Herod's construction, is in the foreground.

were looking for a charge on which they could find Jesus guilty and put him to death. But the witnesses they called did not provide sufficient evidence. So the high priest Caiaphas asked him: "Are you the Messiah, the Son of God?". Jesus replied: "I am."

This they considered to be blasphemy, and the Sanhedrin unanimously agreed was deserving of death. But the Sanhedrin did not have the power to put anyone to death; the death sentence could be passed only by the Roman governor. The governor of Judea was Pontius Pilatus (Pilate). Early on the Friday morning the Jewish authorities roused Pilate and asked him to pass judgement on Jesus. They accused Jesus of treason, urging people not to pay their taxes, calling himself a king and disturbing the peace by his teachings.

Pilate said charges against Jesus were unproved and proposed to let him off with a flogging. Caiaphas warned Pilate that if he did not sentence Jesus he would be "no friend to Caesar" – in other words, Pilate too would be guilty of treason against the emperor. Pilate gave way and sentenced Jesus to death. The sentence was carried out by crucifixion. The Romans reserved it for slaves, the worst criminals and for treason and rebellion.

Because the Sabbath day was due to begin, and with it the Feast of the Passover, the priests asked for Jesus and two thieves crucified with him to be killed before the Sabbath began. In their eyes, the bodies would defile the holy day.

One member of the Sanhedrin, Joseph of Arimathea, asked for Jesus's body and buried it in a new tomb he owned, hewn from the solid rock. A large flat circular stone was rolled across the tomb entrance.

On the Sunday morning two women went to the tomb in order to embalm the body. They found the stone rolled away and the body gone. Later that day, and for several days afterwards, many of Jesus's followers reported having seen and spoken to Jesus. For them, Jesus's return from the dead brought a message of hope for all mankind and was the final indication that the expected Messiah had arrived. It was the basis of the new religion that was to arise from the old traditions of Judaism: Christianity.

It was in a rock-cut tomb like this that Joseph of Arimathea laid the body of Jesus after the Crucifixion. This view is taken from within the tomb. The flat, circular stone which was rolled across the entrance to close it can be seen on the right. This tomb is on the Mount of Olives, near Jerusalem.

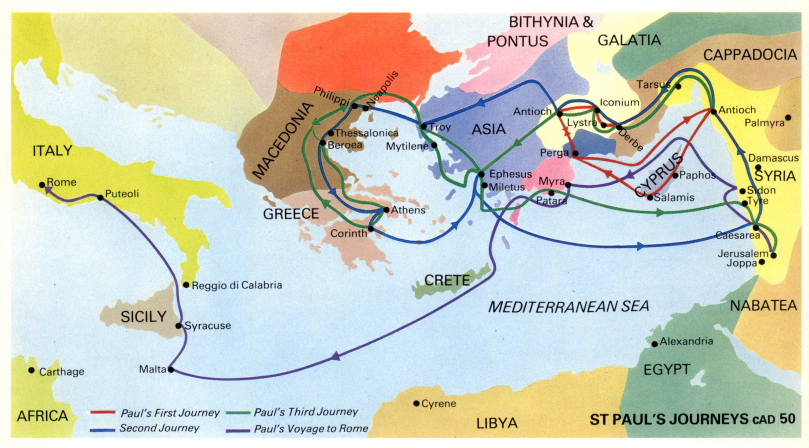

BITHYNIA & PONTUS — GALATIA — CAPPADOCIA

ITALY — Rome — Puteoli

MACEDONIA — Philippi — Neapolis — Thessalonica — Beroea — Troy — Mytilene — ASIA — Antioch — Tarsus — Iconium — Derbe — Lystra — Perga — Antioch — Palmyra

GREECE — Athens — Corinth — Ephesus — Miletus — Myra — Patara — CYPRUS — Paphos — Salamis — SYRIA — Damascus — Sidon — Tyre

Reggio di Calabria — CRETE — MEDITERRANEAN SEA — Caesarea — Jerusalem — Joppa

SICILY — Syracuse — NABATEA

Carthage — Malta — Alexandria — EGYPT

AFRICA — Cyrene — LIBYA

— Paul's First Journey   — Paul's Third Journey
— Second Journey   — Paul's Voyage to Rome

ST PAUL'S JOURNEYS c AD 50

Journeys of the Apostles

Acts of the Apostles

Up to the time of Jesus, the Bible lands were confined to southwestern Asia (in particular Palestine) and Egypt, but after Jesus's crucifixion and resurrection the area involved grows bigger. For the one great idea in the minds of Jesus's followers was to spread the good news that death was not the end, but the beginning and that Jesus lives and is all around you.

The first thing the eleven did was to choose another Apostle to make their numbers up to twelve, following the defection and suicide of Judas Iscariot. They chose Matthias, of whom very little is known.

Paul

Most of the information about the first years of the Christian Church comes from *The Acts of the Apostles*, written by the author of one of the Gospels – Luke. Luke, was a Gentile – that is, a non-Jew. He was also a doctor and the companion of one of the most remarkable people in the history of the Church: Paul.

Paul was a Jew, born and brought up in the city of Tarsus (now in Turkey), where Greek influence was strong. He had also inherited his father's Roman citizenship which saved his life on occasion. It had been granted to his ancestors in 171 BC in return for promoting business in Tarsus.

His Jewish name was Saul, which changed to Paul after he was converted to Christianity. Like other Roman citizens he must have had a second name, but we do not know it. He was trained as a Pharisee, and became a rabbi, or teacher of Jewish law, and like all Jewish men of learning acquired a practical trade, in his case, tent-making.

In the first few years after Jesus's death the Apostles and their followers were fully occupied with preaching the gospel of Jesus and making many converts. The Sanhedrin had the Apostles flogged and ordered them to stop preaching. Of course they continued. Then in AD 36 a Christian preacher named

Stephen was stoned to death by a mob in Jerusalem.

The young rabbi Saul took a leading part in persecuting Christians. On his way to Damascus to arrest any Christians there, Saul had a vision of Jesus and was struck blind. In Damascus he was baptized as a follower of Jesus, recovered his sight and became an ardent preacher of Christianity.

Early Centers of Christianity

The Apostles at first thought that the message of Jesus was for the Jews only. Then Peter baptized a Roman centurion at Caesarea, named Cornelius, and after much debate the Apostles decided that the message of Jesus was for all men, Jews and Gentiles (non-Jews) alike.

This event marked the beginning of the journeys of the Apostles. The greatest traveler of all was Paul, who had retired to his native city of Tarsus for some years. He and a disciple named Barnabas went to Antioch, also in Turkey. It was there that the term "Christian" was first used. The Church at Antioch became an important center for Christianity. Paul and Barnabas set out on a missionary journey in about AD 47. They went first to Cyprus, then to the Roman province of Galatia in north-western Turkey.

Paul's mission was to take the message of Jesus to the Gentiles. His second journey took him to Macedonia, in Greece, then south to Athens and Corinth. In Corinth he fell foul of the orthodox Jews of the city, who tried to persuade Gallio, the Roman proconsul there, to convict him of blasphemy. The charge was dismissed. In Corinth, as elsewhere, Paul seems to have supported himself by making tents.

On his third journey Paul went from Jerusalem to Ephesus, in western Turkey. There he stayed three years and founded a Christian Church, but he upset the silversmiths who profited from the worship at the Greek Temple of Diana.

In AD 58 Paul returned to Jerusalem, where he was saved from an angry mob by Roman troops and imprisoned. They were about to flog him for stirring up trouble when he claimed his Roman citizenship, which carried the right not to be flogged without trial. For two years Paul was in prison in Caesarea and finally appealed to have his case tried by Caesar – the Roman emperor, Nero. So he was sent to Rome. On the way he was shipwrecked in Malta, where he spent three months.

The Bible does not give us further details. According to tradition in AD 63 Paul was tried by Nero and set free. There is a strong tradition that he went to Spain and also returned to Ephesus. Eventually he was arrested, taken back to Rome and beheaded during the intense persecution of Christians which Nero started in AD 64. Peter, also in Rome at this time, was killed too. His grave is believed to be under the mighty basilica of St Peter's in Rome.

Preaching the Gospel Abroad

Of the other Apostles, John is said to have settled in Ephesus, where he died at a great age. There is a strong probability that he either wrote or supplied the information for the Gospel of John. His brother James was executed in Jerusalem by order of Herod Agrippa. Nothing certain is known about his namesake, James the son of Alpheus, or about Matthew, Matthias, or Philip. Tradition says that Andrew traveled in Greece, Bartholomew in Armenia, and Thaddeus (or Jude) and Simon in Persia, while Thomas went to India.

Meanwhile, most of the Roman troops occupying Palestine learned to be careful about the religious feelings of the Jews. Following their Law, the Jews shunned any kind of "graven image". Pontius Pilate, the procurator of Judea who ordered the execution of Jesus, was one of the less tactful Romans, and in AD 36, after many complaints, he was removed from office, though his wife who became a Christian was canonized by the Greek Orthodox Church.

The Martyrdom of St Stephen was painted by the Italian artist Annibale Carracci (1560-1609). It was a popular subject for artists for hundreds of years. Stephen was stoned to death by a mob outside Jerusalem (Acts 7) in the presence of Saul of Tarsus, later the Apostle, Paul. Stephen's death marked the start of a violent persecution of the Christians in Jerusalem.

After the Testaments

Above: The great rock fortress of Masada, on the shores of the Dead Sea. At the north end are the ruins of Herod's palace, while at the west side is the ramp of rock and soil which the Romans built in order to attack Masada in AD 72-73.

Below: The menorah, the seven-branched candlestick from the Temple at Jerusalem, was part of the loot carried off by the Roman general Titus after the Jewish revolt was crushed in AD 70. This relief is on the Arch of Titus in Rome. The arch, completed in AD 82 after Titus became emperor, was built to celebrate his Judean campaign, and one side of it is decorated with carvings of the spoils of war, while the other side portrays the emperor riding in triumph.

ST THOMAS IN INDIA

In the Bible narrative the Apostle Thomas is famous for having refused to believe in Jesus's resurrection until he had both seen and touched him. In later tradition he is claimed to be the founder of the Christians in India. There was already a large Jewish settlement in Bombay at the time of Jesus, so Thomas could well have been sent to preach to the Jews there. A book called *The Acts of Thomas* was written in the AD 200s and tells the story of Thomas's visit to India and his death there. It includes references to King Gondophares, an Indian king who ruled from about AD 19 to AD 45.

Two great events dominate the period immediately after the Bible story comes to an end. One is the *Diaspora*, the final dispersal or scattering of the Jews from Palestine. The other is the steady spread of Christianity in the face of fierce opposition which lasted until the ruler of the empire – Constantine the Great – became a Christian and ended the general persecution of Christians in AD 313.

In AD 41 Herod Agrippa, grandson of Herod the Great, became king of most of Palestine. This was one of the rare examples of wisdom shown by the Emperor Caius (widely known by his nickname of Caligula – "Little Boots"). Caius was more than half mad. Herod Agrippa proved a wise and popular ruler, but he died suddenly after only three years. From then on Judea and most of the rest of Palestine was governed by a succession of procurators, mostly as tactless as Pilatus.

Masada

By AD 66, a full-scale rebellion against the Romans was raging in Judea and Galilee. Beside the Dead Sea a group of Zealots occupied the rock-fortress of Masada, which had been fortified by Herod the Great as a refuge in the event of war. Cestius Gallus, the Imperial Legate in Syria, led an army to crush the rebellion. This army was defeated with the loss of 6000 men.

The Jewish patriots set up a revolutionary government. But they spent much of their time squabbling among themselves instead of preparing for the Roman attack. This came in the spring of AD 67. It was led by two of Rome's best generals, Vespasian (Titus Flavius Sabinus Vespasianus) and his son Titus (who had the same full name). Within a few months they had recaptured the whole of northern Palestine. One of the rebel leaders, Joseph ben Matthias, surrendered to Vespasian and joined the Roman side. He took the Latinized name of Flavius Josephus. He later wrote histories of the Jews and of the wars in which he took part, which are the most valuable sources for the story of those times.

By AD 68 the whole of Palestine, except an area around Jerusalem, was held by the Romans. At this point political troubles in Rome prevented the campaign continuing for a while. During this respite the Jews fought among themselves, moderates against extremists. The Romans resumed their cam-

ATLANTIC OCEAN

Cologne
Mainz
Lyons
Astorga
Saragossa
Merida

Pergamum
Thyatira
Sardis
Smyrna
Philadelphia
Ephesus
Laodicea
PATMOS

BLACK SEA

Salamis
Rome
Naples
Durazzo
Thessalonica
Chalcedon
Develtum
Sinope
Amastris
Ancyra
Troy
Larissa
Nicopolis
Pergamum
Athens
Corinth
Ephesus
Antioch
Perga
Melitene
Edessa
Antioch
Tarsus
Sparta
Hippo Regius
Carthage
Syracuse
Lambaesis
Hadrumetum
Knossos
Salamis
MEDITERRANEAN SEA
Cyrene
Tyre
Damascus
Jerusalem
Alexandria
Memphis

THE SPREAD OF CHRISTIANITY AD 185-325

paign in AD 69. At that point Vespasian, after a year of chaos, as one aspirant after another rose and fell, became Emperor of Rome. So it fell to Titus to complete the conquest. In AD 70 his troops stormed Jerusalem and burned Herod's splendid temple. Only Masada, to the south with a garrison of 960 Zealots held out. After a long siege it faced defeat. So the Zealots decided to kill themselves, rather than be captured alive. Only two women and five children, who hid in a cave, survived.

Diaspora

It might seem that this was the end, but when the fighting stopped, the people began to reconstruct their shattered land. Jerusalem and its Temple remained in ruins, but the religion of Judaism flourished. In AD 115 the Jews in Egypt, Mesopotamia, Cyprus and other areas outside Palestine rebelled against Roman rule. The revolt was crushed with enormous loss of life. Then in AD 132 came the last great revolt of the Jews in Palestine. It was led by Simeon ben Kosiba, known to his followers as Bar-Kokhba – Son of a Star. The rebels took control of Jerusalem and the southern part of Palestine. Bar-Kokhba took the title of president, or prince of Israel. For three years the newly liberated country stayed free.

The Roman governor of Britain, Sextus Julius Severus, was brought over to take charge of the Roman armies. Gradually they recaptured the country, until the rebels were driven to make a last stand at the

mountain fortress of Bethar, which lies southwest of Jerusalem. The Roman armies, by now directed by the Emperor Hadrian, captured it in AD 135. Bar-Kokhba died in battle, and the other Jewish leaders were caught and killed. Judea was laid waste, and no Jews were left there. A few Jewish settlements remained in Galilee. The remaining Jews were dispersed to other lands, the *Diaspora*, as this scattering is known.

The Spread of Christianity

Meanwhile the new religion of Christianity continued to spread. It traveled most quickly within the frontiers of the Roman Empire. Roads and communications within the empire were good. There were also many Jewish settlements and since many of the early members of the Christian Church were Jews they tended to take the Christian message to their fellow people in other lands.

The various Christian communities frequently exchanged visits and letters. Many of these letters survive, but though they tell us a great deal about the spiritual state of the Church they do not say much about how quickly it spread.

At first the center of Christianity remained at Jerusalem, though there were important churches in Antioch, Ephesus and elsewhere. But during the war of AD 66-70 the Christians left, and by the second century AD the two main centers were Alexandria and Rome. Gradually Rome, as the place where Peter and Paul were martyred, became the heart of Christendom.

The spread of Christianity is shown here over a period of about 300 years. In the lightest area people were following Christianity by AD 185; the next area shows how Christianity had spread by AD 325. The darkest area indicates the non-Christian portion of the world in AD 325. The small panel indicates the area enlarged top right, showing the "seven churches in the province of Asia" to whom John wrote his Revelation. The Transfiguration of Christ, bottom left, is from a Byzantine mosaic of the AD 500s in the Monastery of St Catherine on Mount Sinai.

Time Chart

Many of the early dates in this Time Chart are only approximate, but they do show the relationship between events in the Bible, and those recorded elsewhere.

BC

c 4000	Flood overwhelmed Ur.
c 1900	Abraham.
c 1730	Hyksos kings conquered Egypt.
c 1580	End of Hyksos rule.
c 1292	Rameses II, Pharaoh of Egypt. The Exodus.
c 1150-1025	Period of the Judges.
c 1025	Saul became king.
c 1000	David became king.
c 961	Solomon became king.
c 922	Solomon's kingdom split into Judah and Israel.
c 918	Pharaoh Sheshonk I invaded Palestine.
876-869	Omri king of Israel.
869-850	Ahab king of Israel.
842-815	Jehu king of Israel.
786-746	Jeroboam II, king of Israel.
783-742	Uzziah, king of Judah.
715-687	Hezekiah, king of Judah.
722/1	Assyrians conquered Israel.
605-562	Nebuchadnezzar, king of Babylon.
597	Babylonians invaded Judah: many Jews deported.
586	Fall of Jerusalem; destruction of Solomon's Temple: main deportation of Jews.
539	Cyrus II of Persia conquered Babylon.
538	End of the Babylon captivity.
444	Nehemiah, governor of Judea.
432	Nehemiah's second visit to Judea.
362	Phoenicians revolted against Persians.
335	Darius III, king of Persia.
333	Battle of Issus: Alexander the Great conquered Persian empire.
323	Death of Alexander the Great: break-up of his empire.
320	Ptolemy, ruler of Egypt, invaded Palestine.
198	Antiochus III of Syria conquered Palestine.
168	Revolt of the Jews, led by the Maccabees.
165	Jerusalem recaptured: worship in the Temple restored.
160	Death of Judas Maccabeus.
160-142	Jonathan Maccabeus ruled Judea.
142-134	Simon Maccabeus ruled Judea.
134-105	John Hyrcanus ruled Judea.
129	Judea freed from Syrian rule.
63	Pompey conquered Palestine for Rome.
37	Herod the Great, king of Judea under the Romans.
27	Octavius Caesar effectively became the first Roman emperor, Augustus.
c 6	Most widely accepted date of the birth of Jesus of Nazareth at Bethlehem.
4	Death of Herod the Great; Palestine divided among his sons.

AD

26	Pontius Pilatus appointed procurator of Judea.
c 33	Crucifixion of Jesus.
36	Pontius Pilatus dismissed; Stephen stoned to death; Saul (Paul) of Tarsus converted.
41-44	Herod Agrippa I, king of Judea.
c 47	Paul's first missionary journey.
52	Paul tried before Gallio at Corinth.
c 58	Paul returned to Jerusalem.
c 60	Paul sent to Rome for trial.
c 63	Paul tried by Nero and freed.
64	Nero began persecution of Christians in Rome.
	Probable date of Peter's martyrdom in Rome.
66	Revolt of the Jews began.
c 67	Paul martyred in Rome.
70	Destruction of Jerusalem and Herod's temple.
73	Fall of Masada.
115	Revolt of Jews outside Palestine.
132	Revolt of Simeon Bar-Kokhba.
135	Judea laid waste; final dispersal of the Jews.

ACKNOWLEDGEMENTS

Sonia Halliday Photos:
Sonia Halliday/Laura Lushington, Cover & endpapers, Page 6 bottom, Page 7 bottom, Page 9, Page 12, Page 14, Page 15, Page 17, Page 21, Page 24, Page 36, Page 39, Page 40. Peter Marsden: Page 6 top. Jane Taylor: Page 11 center, Page 19, Page 23 bottom, Page 30 bottom, Page 34, Page 37. James Wellard: Page 31 top. F. H. C. Birch: Page 42 bottom.

British Museum: page 11 top, Page 7 top. Peter Clayton: Page 26. Michael Holford: Page 28. Israel Tourist Office: Page 35, Page 42. Mansell Collection: Page 32. National Gallery: Page 41. Ronald Sheridan Library: Page 23 bottom.

Index